The Camping
Bible

Bob Holtzman

The Camping Bible

THE ESSENTIAL GUIDE FOR OUTDOOR ENTHUSIASTS

Bob Holtzman

CHARTWELL
BOOKS, INC.

Conceived, designed, and produced by
Quid Publishing
Level 4 Sheridan House
114 Western Road
Hove BN3 1DD
www.quidpublishing.com

Cover photo © Mikael Damkier / Shutterstock

This edition published in 2013 by
CHARTWELL BOOKS, INC.
A division of BOOK SALES, INC.
276 Fifth Avenue Suite 206
New York, New York 10001
USA

ISBN-13: 978-0-7858-2983-6

Printed in China

1 3 5 7 9 10 8 6 4 2

Every effort has been made to ensure that all of the information in this book is correct at
the time of publication. This book is not intended to replace manufacturers' instructions
in the use of their products—always follow their safety guidelines. The author, publisher,
and copyright holder assume no responsibility for any injury, loss, or damage caused or
sustained as a consequence of the use and application of the contents of this book.

This one is for:
– volunteers everywhere who care for wild places and things
– the folks who have taught me how to enjoy and thrive in the wilderness
– and Max, who needs to come canoeing with me again soon.

CONTENTS

Introduction

Camping is a lot like writing, painting, golf, public speaking, playing the saxophone, and just about any other endeavor that involves skill and experience: the more you do it, the better you'll get and the more you'll enjoy it.

Until you actually set up that tent and feel what it's like to sleep outdoors in a sleeping bag, it's all just theory and unfulfilled dreams. As useful as this book is, there's no substitute for the real thing. So, the most essential piece of advice to impart is to simply get going!

Start small. **Make your first camping trip a two- or three-day affair fairly close to home**. Forget about climbing Denali until you have the basics under your belt. Instead, enjoy the convenience and safety of a nearby state park. Do this just three or four times and you'll gain substantial insight into your own capabilities and what you'd enjoy for your next camping experience.

When starting out, **rent or borrow as much of the essential equipment as you can** rather than buying it. Again, just a little experience will serve to teach you a great deal about your needs and preferences when it comes to clothing choices, tent designs, backpack and stove types, and other gear.

Although it's not essential, **taking your first camping trip with experienced campers is highly recommended**. Join a local camping club or a regional or national outdoors organization with a local chapter, and sign up for one of their organized trips. You will find friendly people who are eager to welcome newcomers to the world of camping with good advice and good fellowship.

Get to know the gear gurus at your local outfitter. These folks want to see happy campers, and they'll rarely steer you wrong or try to sell you stuff you don't need. They want you to be excited about camping and pleased with your gear purchase so that you'll come back for more. They're also a great source of information about local camping clubs, parks, and trails.

Planning is an essential aspect of camping. Well . . . almost essential. The more experience you gain, the less you'll need to depend upon checklists and rigid procedures. Some of the best short trips are spur of the moment, when you notice an intriguing-looking green area on the map and say to yourself "Let's go see what's there."

That said, it's foolish not to plan your trip when you have the time to do so. Since you're reading this book, you obviously appreciate the value of careful preparation, and that's the subject of **Part 1**. You'll learn how to select a camping destination, choose a good time to go, and make other preparations for your first trip or your fiftieth.

In **Part 2**, this book looks at camping equipment: tents and sleeping bags, stoves and backpacks, clothing and footwear, tools for navigation, signaling, and lots more. It examines the types of gear that are appropriate to backpacking, bicycle camping, car and RV camping, and boat camping. As the popularity of ultralight backpacking shows, it's possible to enjoy camping with a minimum of gear. So don't let gear prices scare you off, and don't delay your first camping experience because you don't own everything that someone else says you need.

Part 3 covers camping skills and techniques: how to pack your gear and food, make and break camp, build a fire, prepare and clean up after a meal, obtain safe drinking water, and more. Among the most important information in this part are practices meant to safeguard the environment. Many camping areas are heavily used, requiring everyone to be on the honor system to leave the place in as good a shape as you find it. As mealtime plays a central role in any camping day, some favorite camping recipes are included.

The chances of being attacked by a bear or buried in an avalanche are really quite slim, and with a little bit of knowledge and preparation, you can keep them that way. That's the objective of **Part 4**: Hazards, which covers not only these extremely rare life-threatening disasters, but also more common problems like mosquitoes and poison ivy. There's brief discussion of first aid for some common camping injuries and illnesses, but please don't mistake this book for a comprehensive resource on wilderness medicine.

Part 5 looks at backpacking and hiking skills, including land navigation, walking skills for difficult terrain, and the important subject of taking care of your feet when you're depending upon them for round-trip transportation into and out of the wilderness.

Kids get into the act in **Part 6**, which discusses how to keep them enthusiastic and safe and how to make them a cooperative part of the camping endeavor. Keep it fun for them, keep it interesting, and keep them well-fed (you'll find several fun recipes for kids to prepare themselves), and you may find camping to be the very best thing you do as a family.

But above all, get going! Don't wait for your honeymoon, or the right tent, or your kids to get older, or yourself to gain an exhaustive knowledge of wild foods. The outdoors is waiting for you. Go enjoy it now.

1 PLANNING

What Kind of Camping

How you get there has a huge influence on your camping experience. Drive your car or recreational vehicle (RV) right onto the campsite, and almost everything about your trip—what you see, what you eat, who you meet, and what you do for fun—will be different than if you hike in, or arrive by bicycle or canoe. The differences are so pronounced, in fact, that most styles of camping are defined by the method of transportation used.

BACKPACKING

Backpacking is the classic camping experience. You leave roads and crowds behind and stride into the wilderness with everything you need on your back.

This also means that you have to be able to carry everything you need. Once you've packed your tent, sleeping bag, cooking gear, food, and a few other bare necessities into your backpack, there's little space left for luxuries, and every additional pound is literally a burden. Much of the appeal of backpacking comes from paring things down to their essentials to experience life and nature at their most basic, elemental levels.

Close to Nature

That makes nature the primary attraction. Depending upon where you hike, you'll spend days or weeks amid trees and birds, streams and mountains, forest or desert scenery. You don't have to be a trained naturalist to appreciate what you see, but a little knowledge of the natural world will make the experience more fulfilling. For that reason, nature field guides are among the most common extra-weight "luxuries" that backpackers carry.

Health and Fitness

The essence of backpacking, though, is walking. Backpackers should be committed pedestrians, because it's really about the journey, not the destination.

More than most other modes of camping, backpacking requires physical fitness. When planning a backpacking trip, it's a good idea to consult a physician to ensure that you're up to the challenge. If you're out of shape, several weeks of physical training can prepare you for the experience. The best practice for hiking is hiking. If you're largely sedentary, start walking to build up your strength and endurance.

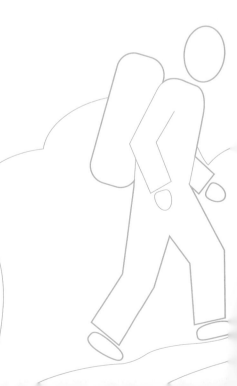

Most long-distance hikers lose weight on the trail. If that's your objective, great! But it also means that you have to pay close attention to nutrition, to keep your body strong and healthy when it's working hard. Proper foot care is essential, as blisters can be truly debilitating. You'll also have to be prepared to cope with extremes of weather and (hopefully) minor medical incidents on your own.

Backpacking Gear

Many campers maintain a love–hate relationship with their gear, and none more so than backpackers. There's pleasure to be had in owning and using a nice piece of equipment, but good camping gear is often costly. Backpackers naturally prefer lightweight gear, which tends to be even more expensive. Finding that sweet spot, where weight, price, and quality are all in balance, is a personal decision, based on the strength of your back, the size of your pocketbook, and your willingness to accept a product failure in the field.

Backpacking requires physical fitness and that you pare your gear to a minimum.

Planning

Gear

Techniques

Hazards

Hiking

Camping with Kids

CAR CAMPING

Camping out of your car is a fundamentally different experience than backpacking. Where backpackers head down a foot trail and make camp in a remote site, car campers drive into a campground and park on the campsite, often just a couple yards from other campsites occupied by other car or RV campers.

Drive-in campgrounds may be public or private (i.e., government-run or commercial), but most offer comforts and amenities unavailable to backpackers. At minimum, this usually means clean flush toilets, hot showers, a picnic table, and a barbecue grill, but it may also include electrical hookups, wireless internet, sand beaches with lifeguards, canoe rentals, volleyball courts, and a clubhouse with DVDs, table tennis, and nightly activities.

Most car campers use tents that are more spacious (and heavier) than the ones carried by backpackers. Likewise, you can bring a big, comfy air mattress or even a cot. You'll cook in the open but there's no need to subsist on dehydrated meals prepared on a tiny backpacking stove. You can bring a multi-burner stove or a charcoal grill, a cooler full of ice and fresh food, and "normal" cookware and dishware.

Car camping isn't the "all-natural" experience of backpacking, but it has its advantages. For families with young children, it's a soft entry into the camping experience. Especially if backpacking seems too strenuous, it's a great way to spend time outdoors and away from your usual haunts. For some, car camping is just a way to avoid paying expensive hotel rates when taking a "regular" vacation. You can leave the tent set up in the campground and drive into town to visit relatives, theme parks, or cultural attractions.

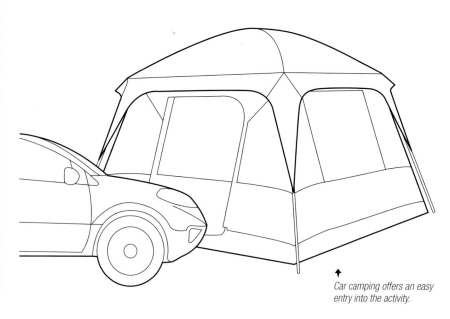

Car camping offers an easy entry into the activity.

RVING

It's tempting to put quotation marks around "camping" when discussing recreational vehicles. You sleep under a solid roof in something very much like a regular bed. You cook on a regular stove or use a microwave oven. You can plug the vehicle into a power pylon and enjoy air conditioning and television. You don't even have to leave your shelter to use the toilet or take a shower.

Still, RV enthusiasts call it camping, and they undoubtedly stay in campgrounds, so let's give RVing its due. It has all the advantages of car camping plus greater comfort and carrying capacity. (A big disadvantage is fuel mileage. It costs a lot more to drive an RV rig than a car.) There's virtually nothing you can do at home that you can't do in an RV. Acknowledging this explicitly, self-propelled RVs are even *called* motorhomes.

Stay or Go?

What RVers give up to nature, they get back in community. RV campgrounds are decidedly social places, especially among retirees who make up a large percentage of the RV fraternity. Stays tend to be long, lasting for weeks or even months. It's not unusual for these sedentary RVers to plant gardens and set up lawn decorations and elaborate outdoor seating and dining arrangements where friends gather nightly for cards and cocktails.

Other RVers are constantly on the move, spending just a night or two in a campground and then moving on to another. This is a great way to see the country. But if you add up the cost of fuel, campground fees, and RV ownership or rental, it's not necessarily cheaper than traveling by car and staying in motels.

RVs provide campers with all the comforts of home.

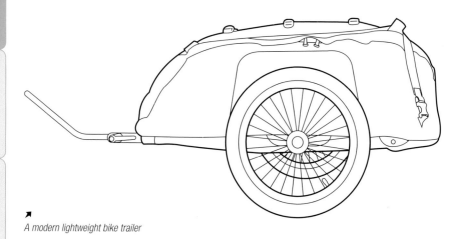

A modern lightweight bike trailer

BIKE CAMPING

Like backpacking, bicycle camping requires that you really like the mode of travel. Be prepared to spend many hours in the saddle, some of them in miserable weather. Also like car and RV camping, most bike camping occurs on a drive-in campsite, close to other campers in a busy vehicular campground.

However, bike camping is quite unlike backpacking and car/RV camping in some respects. Bike campers tend to be goal-oriented and, as much as they like to ride, trips almost always have clear destinations. Bike campers enjoy neither the comforts of car-camping nor the natural beauty and solitude that backpackers experience. For many cyclists, camping is a necessary evil— what they do when they're not riding or enjoying the destination.

Bike Camping Gear

Cycling places a premium on weight and volume, so cyclists use much the same camping gear as backpackers: tiny, lightweight tents, stoves, and cooksets, lightweight foods, and little else. Clothing and footwear are designed for the specific physical dynamics of cycling. Cyclists must also carry tools and spares to maintain their rides. As breakdowns are not uncommon, at least one rider in every group should be a competent mechanic.

Gear is carried in *panniers*—bags that mount beside the rear, and often the front, wheels. A less popular but viable alternative is to haul your gear on a trailer.

Supported Trips

Tour operators offer *supported* bike trips in which a van carries the cyclists' personal gear, plus tents, kitchen sets, food, tools, and spares. Cyclists carry only a snack, a beverage, and perhaps a spare piece of outerwear, and meet the "sag wagon" at prearranged lunch stops and campgrounds, where the tour operator does the cooking.

BOAT CAMPING

Camping out of a canoe, kayak, or inflatable river raft combines backpacking's opportunities for remote wilderness experience with cargo-carrying capacity that can approach that of car-camping. Like backpacking and cycling, much of the joy of boat camping is in the mode of travel.

The carrying capacity of a canoe allows you to bring a larger tent, a more substantial cookset, and more food than is possible in a backpack, making lengthy trips possible without resupply. Kayaks typically carry less gear than canoes but far more than backpacks. Some river rafts can carry as much gear as a good-size car. Few backpackers cook over open fires anymore, but many boat-campers do, because they can afford the extra weight of an axe or saw. It's a natural to carry fishing gear, making fresh fish a particular pleasure of boat camping.

Boating Skills

More than any other form of camping, boat camping demands special skills. We all know how to walk, and most of us know how to drive a car and ride a bike. But anyone who heads down a river with a canoe full of gear and no knowledge of boat handling is asking for trouble. So while someone who has never backpacked, bike-camped, or car-camped could probably have a good, safe time on his or her first trip with no more guidance than this book, the same is not true for the inexperienced boater.

Training is essential. The best way to get it is through one of the official sanctioning organizations, like the American Canoe Association (ACA) or the British Canoe Union (BCU), or through an outdoor-training organization like Outward Bound. Many nature organizations, canoe and kayak clubs, YMCAs, and private outfitters also offer ACA-certified training. Failing those, receiving paddling instruction from experienced paddlers, and then taking several trips in their company, may impart the necessary skills.

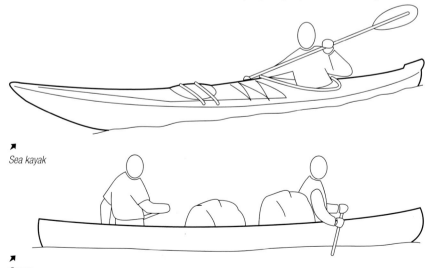

↗
Sea kayak

↗
Canoe

Where to Camp

Planning

Rustic or luxurious? Secluded or public? Mountains or plains, forest, desert, or seashore? Deciding where to camp involves these choices and others. Whether you camp in your home town or in a different hemisphere, location does much to determine the nature of your camping experience.

TYPES OF CAMPSITES

In remote wilderness areas accessible only by hikers or canoeists, campsites are basic and rustic. A small patch of cleared ground provides a space to pitch a tent. There is often a fire ring, sometimes a rough picnic table and, 100 feet or so down a side trail, an outhouse with a plank seat over a hole in the ground. That's about it. There's a reason it's called "roughing it."

At the opposite end of the spectrum are fully equipped campgrounds that cater primarily to RVers. Individual campsites may be large enough to park a motorhome the size of a city bus, with a "pull-through" layout so that you never have to back your vehicle in or out. Beside the carefully leveled parking pad is an electrical hookup. A spigot provides potable water to your home-on-wheels (you'll need your own hose), and there might be a connection to a sewer system. (If not, then there's likely a central "dumping station" where RVs can empty their holding tanks.) On the loop road that connects all the campsites, there might even be streetlights! And then there's the clubhouse, shower building, outdoor recreation facilities, and maybe a store where you can restock your fridge, rent a DVD, and buy repair parts for your vehicle.

In between is a continuum of campsites and campgrounds offering more or less luxury and more or less of a wilderness experience. "Group sites" are set aside for larger groups, typically with six to ten tents and 12 to 20 individuals; "dispersed sites" are restricted to just one or two tents and four to six individuals, and are usually out of sight and earshot of each other. Some hiking trails offer huts instead of tent sites, and these range from log lean-tos that offer just a platform and a roof to log cabins with electric power, stone fireplaces, and flush toilets. Backpack-only sites may be ugly and crowded or might offer the same amenities as the lushest RV park. RV campgrounds can be run-down and dirty, or might offer nicely secluded campsites that put you in close contact with nature and natural beauty.

The only way to be sure of staying in the kind of campsite you want is to do research before leaving home. We'll cover sources of information on pages 36–37.

WHO RUNS IT?

Camping areas are run by a wide range of organizations. At the top of the list is the U.S. government, which allows various types of camping on lands managed by the National Parks Service, the National Forest Service, the Bureau of Land Management, and several other agencies. (See Resources, page 183 for contact information for these and other camping facilities.)

Camping on federal lands runs the gamut from well-equipped RV campgrounds in famous locations like Grand Canyon National Park in Arizona and Acadia National Park in Maine, to desolate badlands like New Mexico's Bisti/De-Na-Zin Wilderness, where the Bureau of Land Management allows camping, but provides no facilities whatsoever and the basic policy is "camp

Gear

Techniques

Hazards

Hiking

Camping with Kids

where you want to and try not to die." Obviously, anyone heading into such a harsh and isolated area must be well-equipped and experienced. Just because it's run by the federal government is no guarantee that it's safe for beginners, and you *can't* count on the Feds coming to bail you out if you happen to get into trouble.

Every state also maintains campgrounds and natural areas with ranges of amenities, as do some counties and municipalities.

While most private campgrounds focus on the automotive camper, they are as diverse in their quality, beauty, and amenities as public sites. Best known are national chains like KOA Kampgrounds and Encore RV Resorts, but a far larger number are single-site mom-and-pop operations that set their own standards. Campgrounds inside the big national parks are often booked solid, but there's usually a private operation nearby

ready to pick up the overflow and often offering excellent access to the major sites at more attractive prices. It's not unusual for a private campground to offer private lake access for swimming or fishing, trails for day-hiking, and a nicer overall experience (better views, less crowding) than the government-run campground next door.

Camping on private land isn't always of the drive-in variety. Many large landowners—especially timberland owners, environmental organizations, and hunting and fishing clubs—open up their lands to hikers or canoeists either year-round or at particular times of the year. These facilities aren't quite so easy to find as the ones run by government agencies, but a call to a local outfitter or a forest-service field office can often uncover opportunities that aren't listed in most guidebooks or directories.

↗
RV camping

Planning

Gear

Techniques

Hazards

Hiking

Camping with Kids

CAMPING BY REGION

Take your first few camping trips close to home. You've got more than enough to do figuring out what gear to buy, planning your first camping menu, and learning how to set up your tent without adding the difficulties of long-distance travel. Your first camping trip will expose you to so many new experiences that there's just no need to add the novelty of a distant location to make it fun, fulfilling, and somewhat challenging. Another advantage of camping close to home: you know what kind of weather to expect, and you already own most of the right clothing. (Remember what Henry David Thoreau said on this topic: "Beware of all enterprises that require new clothes.")

Once you have a few trips under your belt, you'll be ready for the additional challenge of unfamiliar territory. We live in a vast and varied country, and travel between the U.S. and Canada is so easy that intrepid campers should consider both to be wide-open for the purposes of planning an adventure. What follows are some of the highlights.

Northeast

Topping out at a little over 6,000 feet, Eastern mountains are mere bumps compared to the Rockies, but they offer great woodlands hiking, and a few of them peek above the treeline. Two fantastic backpacking destinations are the White Mountain National Forest in New Hampshire and Maine, and New York's Adirondack Park—the largest state park in the country. Acadia National Park on Mount Desert Island, Maine, offers the unusual juxtaposition of mountains descending right to the sea and the only fjords in the Northeast. The Cape Cod National Seashore offers lighthouses and other historic sites and miles of sand beaches. The nonprofit-managed Maine Island Trail is sea-kayakers' heaven, with dozens of isolated campsites on rocky, sparsely inhabited islands off Maine coast.

Unless you're prepared for cold weather and even snow, camping in the Northeast is generally restricted to May through October. Mosquitoes and black flies can be a problem early in the season, but they taper off as summer progresses. By the time the leaves turn to their awesome fall colors, the season is just about over for warm-weather campers.

Mid-Atlantic

On the border between New Jersey and Pennsylvania, where the Delaware River cuts through the Appalachian Mountains, is the Delaware Water Gap National Recreation Area, prime canoeing, rafting, and hiking territory. Several New Jersey state parks offer camping in the midst of the Pinelands (also known as the Pine Barrens): covered with stunted scrubby pines, it's a slightly eerie, sparsely populated coastal plain surprisingly close to New York City and Philadelphia. The beautiful Skyline Drive cuts through Shenandoah National Park in Virginia, just 75 miles from Washington, DC. Virginia also features the longest section of the Appalachian Trail, a 2,184-mile hiking path that runs from Georgia to Maine. Campers on Assateague Island National Seashore, Maryland, are often treated to the sight of herds of rare wild ponies roaming the beaches.

Mid-Atlantic campers have more months of pleasant weather than the Northeast, although muggy weather in July and August can make hiking seem like a steam bath.

Northeast

Mid-Atlantic

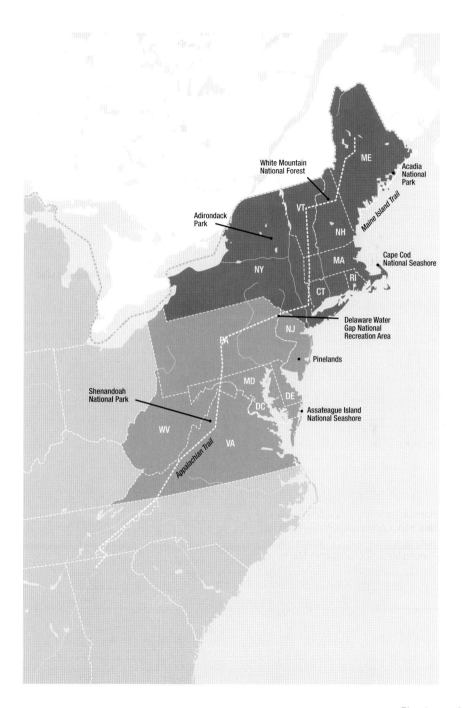

White Mountain
National Forest

Adirondack
Park

Acadia
National
Park

ME

Maine Island Trail

VT

NH

Cape Cod
National Seashore

MA

NY

RI

CT

Delaware Water
Gap National
Recreation Area

NJ

PA

Pinelands

MD

DC

DE

Shenandoah
National Park

Assateague Island
National Seashore

WV

VA

Appalachian Trail

Planning

Gear

Techniques

Hazards

Hiking

Camping with Kids

Southeast

Noted for the diversity of its plant- and wildlife, the Great Smoky Mountains National Park in North Carolina and Tennessee gets more visitors than any other national park. Notable for its miles of interconnected caverns, Cumberland Gap National Historic Park commemorates the opening of the American "west"—in this early case, Kentucky. Sandstone gorges and bluffs provide excellent opportunities for whitewater rafting, horseback riding, mountain biking, and hiking in the Big South Fork National River and Recreation Area in Kentucky and Tennessee. Florida's Everglades National Park and the adjacent Big Cypress National Preserve provide access to unique ecosystems of mangroves, sawgrass, tropical hardwood hammocks, alligators, and the endangered Florida panther.

Weather in this subtropical zone can range from warm in winter to stiflingly hot and humid in summer. Rain can be expected year-round, and this moist weather means that mosquitoes and other insect pests are a near-constant fact of life in many areas.

Midwest and Central

Many of the finest camping opportunities in the Midwest involve major bodies of water. Michigan's Isle Royale National Park consists of the largest island in Lake Superior and hundreds of smaller ones, and is easily reached by ferry or float plane. Explore sea caves and lighthouses in the Apostle Islands National Lakeshore in Wisconsin, also on Lake Superior. The Boundary Waters Canoe Area Wilderness in northern Minnesota offers fine fishing and extensive canoe tripping opportunities on hundreds of lakes, along with a taste of the region's French *voyageur* history. Things are more dramatic, less lovely, and a lot drier in the Theodore Roosevelt National Park, located in the North Dakota Badlands, a habitat for wild horses, bison, elk, and bighorn sheep.

The Soldier Creek Wilderness, part of the Pine Ridge section of the Nebraska National Forest, is a top ecotourism destination, with opportunities for camping, deer hunting and fishing amidst ponderosa pine forest. Missouri's Lake of the Ozarks State Park offers miles of ATV trails through thousands of acres of woodlands, along with cave tours, rock climbing, swimming beaches, bridle trails and a boats-only aquatic trail. Kanopolis State Park belies the notion that Kansas is nothing but cornfields: there are praries, canyons, and forested areas, with hundreds of drive-in and hike-in campsites, trails for mountain biking and horseback riding, beaches, cabins, and a marina.

Big Bend National Park, on the Texas border with Mexico, protects an area of the Chihuahuan Desert and offers backpackers great hiking trails with remarkable geology, an abundance of wildlife, and ancient cultural sites.

Summers are warm and humid in the upper Midwest and Great Lakes and harsh in winter. Temperatures are more extreme in the Great Plains, where rainfall is sparse and high winds blow almost year-round, sometimes generating dust storms that can range from merely annoying to dangerous. Tornadoes are another weather hazard particular to the Great Plains.

Southeast

Midwest and Central

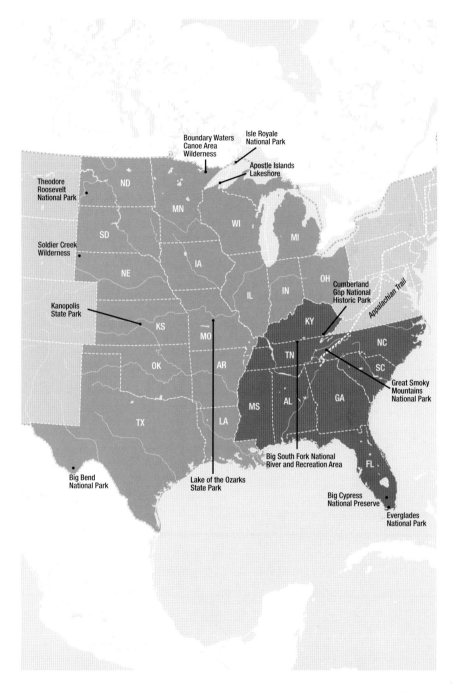

Theodore
Roosevelt
National Park

Soldier Creek
Wilderness

Kanopolis
State Park

Big Bend
National Park

Boundary Waters
Canoe Area
Wilderness

Isle Royale
National Park

Apostle Islands
Lakeshore

Cumberland
Gap National
Historic Park

Great Smoky
Mountains
National Park

Big South Fork National
River and Recreation Area

Lake of the Ozarks
State Park

Big Cypress
National Preserve

Everglades
National Park

Appalachian Trail

ND
MN
WI
MI
SD
IA
NE
OH
IL
IN
KY
KS
MO
NC
OK
AR
TN
SC
MS
AL
GA
TX
LA
FL

Planning

Gear

Techniques

Hazards

Hiking

Camping with Kids

Northwest

Grand Teton National Park in Wyoming offers serious mountaineering opportunities with glorious views from mountain bases as well as peaks. Just ten miles away is Yellowstone National Park, famous for its geysers, hot springs, waterfalls, and other dramatic geology. Although the active glaciers in Montana's Glacier National Park are retreating rapidly (apparently due to climate change), the park still offers spectacular Rocky Mountain trail hiking and climbing and an abundance of wildlife. Crater Lake National Park in Oregon centers on an extinct volcano that encircles one of the world's deepest lakes. Passing through the park is the Pacific Crest Trail, the West's answer to the Adirondack Trail, stretching 2,650 miles from the Canadian to the Mexican borders.

Coastal areas of the Northwest have generally mild temperatures year-round, but rain is a given in winter months. Altitude has a huge effect on temperatures, and campers in mountain regions should be prepared for cool days and below-freezing nights even during the height of summer. Snow makes some mountain hiking trails impassable during all but a few months of the year.

Southwest

Sitting astride the Continental Divide in Colorado, Rocky Mountain National Park offers outdoor enthusiasts opportunities for everything from RV camping to mountaineering and big-wall rock climbing, with backpacking and horsepacking thrown in for good measure. Thousands of natural sandstone arches, as well as spires, balancing rocks, and eroded monoliths are the main attraction in Arches National Park in Utah, while the nearby Canyonlands National Park features equally fascinating geology in the form of buttes, mesas, and canyons carved by the Colorado and Green rivers. Salt flats, sand dunes, badlands, valleys, canyons, and mountains all come together in California

and Nevada in Death Valley National Park, the largest national park in the contiguous 48 states. Camping opportunities also exist in California's Yosemite and Joshua Tree national parks and, of course, in Arizona's incomparable Grand Canyon.

Rain is rarely a problem in the desert, of course, but daytime temperatures commonly exceed 100°F throughout the summer. Nonetheless, be prepared for the mercury to drop rapidly when the sun goes down. Southwest campers must also beware of forest fires, lightning storms, and flash floods. On the plus side? No mosquitoes!

Alaska and Hawaii

Denali National Park and Preserve in Alaska contains North America's highest mountain (the peak of Denali, also known as Mt. McKinley, is 20,320 feet above sea level) and a wealth of Arctic wildlife, including caribou, grizzly and black bears, ptarmigan, Dall sheep, moose, and wolverines. Alaskan weather varies greatly, depending primarily upon proximity to the sea (a moderating factor) and elevation. Some areas are quite dry, while others receive as much as 100 inches of precipitation annually. During the summer, mosquitoes are unspeakably bad in low elevations and night-time darkness is brief. Winter, of course, is incredibly harsh.

Ever think about camping on a volcano? Hawaii Volcanoes National Park has hiking trails on both the world's largest and most active ones. Near-constant trade winds give Hawaii its beautiful tropical climate, but be prepared for cool temperatures if you climb a volcano. Rain falls almost daily from October to April.

 Northwest   *Alaska and Hawaii*

 Southwest

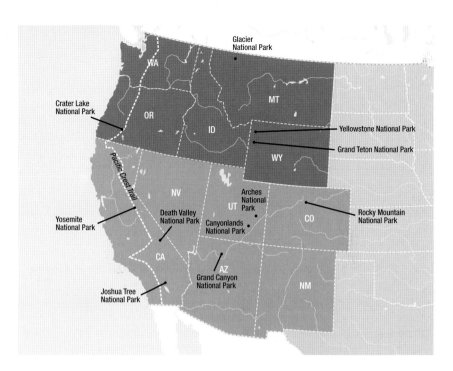

Glacier
National Park

Crater Lake
National Park

Pacific Crest Trail

Yellowstone National Park

Grand Teton National Park

Arches
National
Park

Rocky Mountain
National Park

Yosemite
National Park

Death Valley
National Park

Canyonlands
National Park

Joshua Tree
National Park

Grand Canyon
National Park

WA

MT

OR

ID

WY

NV

UT

CO

CA

AZ

NM

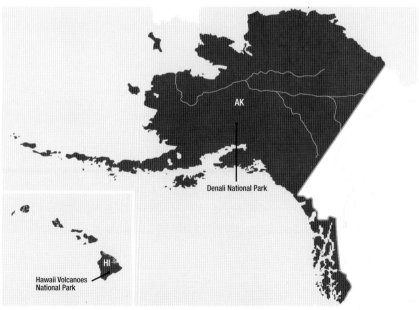

AK

Denali National Park

Hawaii Volcanoes
National Park

HI

Planning

Gear

Techniques

Hazards

Hiking

Camping with Kids

Eastern Canada

Two very different landscapes dominate Newfoundland's Gros Morne National Park: a coastal lowland on the Gulf of St. Lawrence, and an inland zone of alpine plateau and mountains. Combined, these encompass temperate, boreal and arctic environments with diverse biological communities. Famous for its cliffs overlooking the Atlantic Ocean, Cape Breton Highlands National Park in Nova Scotia features great backpacking and scenic fishing villages along the 185-mile Cabot Trail. Prince Edward Island National Park boasts beaches, dunes, wetlands, forests, and the farmhouse that served as the setting for L.M. Montgomery's *Anne of Green Gables*.

Forillon National Park, on Quebec's Gaspé Peninsula, is a geologist's playground, with ten distinct rock formations, along with seabird colonies, arctic and alpine flora, and the Grande-Grave National Heritage Site, preserving the history of the area's fishing communities. Kouchibouguac National Park in New Brunswick offers camping via bicycle, canoe, kayak, and on foot amidst a patchwork of salt marshes, forests, sand dunes, bogs, rivers, and lagoons.

Close to Montreal and Toronto amidst the Thousand Islands is the St. Lawrence Islands National Park. Most of the park's campsites are accessible only by boat. Ontario's Algonquin Provincial Park, with more than 2,400 lakes, virtually guarantees great fishing, wildlife viewing (including bear, beaver, wolf and loon), and solitude. Another superb Ontario canoeing destination is Quetico Provincial Park, adjacent to the Boundary Waters Canoe Area Wilderness in Minnesota; in many ways, the two areas function as a single international park. Think twice before visiting Auyuittuq National Park, on Nunavut's Baffin Island. With its harsh arctic conditions, sparse vegetation, and resident polar bears, this park is a serious challenge for all but the most experienced.

Western Canada

Grasslands, upland boreal forests and eastern deciduous forests come together in Manitoba's Riding Mountain National Park. Among its highlights are the Ochre River Trail (used by backpackers, horsepackers, mountain bikers and cross-country skiers) and its wildlife (including bison, moose, elk, wolves, black bear, and hundreds of bird species). Visitors to Prince Albert National Park in Saskatchewan enjoy hiking trails, fishing, canoeing, the Stanley Thompson-designed Waskesiu Golf Course, and the cabin once owned by naturalist-author Grey Owl, on Ajawaan Lake.

Set in the high Rocky Mountains, Alberta's Banff National Park is easily reached by rail and the Trans-Canada Highway. More than five million come here annually to camp, hike, climb, fish, and view glaciers, icefields and mountain peaks along the Continental Divide. Larger than Switzerland, the Wood Buffalo National Park, on Alberta's northern boreal plains, is home to huge herds of bison and the world's only natural nesting area for whooping cranes.

Pacific Rim National Park Reserve on Vancouver Island, British Columbia, has three main divisions: the Long Beach area includes sandy beaches, bogs, and temperate rainforest; the Broken Islands are popular among kayak campers; and the West Coast Trail is a rugged hike through bogs and old-growth rainforest, and across rocky beaches. Well above the Arctic Circle on Banks Island in the Northwest Territories is Aulavik National Park. Large herds of musk oxen and the endangered Peary caribou live here amidst polar deserts and badlands and in the valley of the canoe-navigable Thomsen River.

 Eastern Canada

 Western Canada

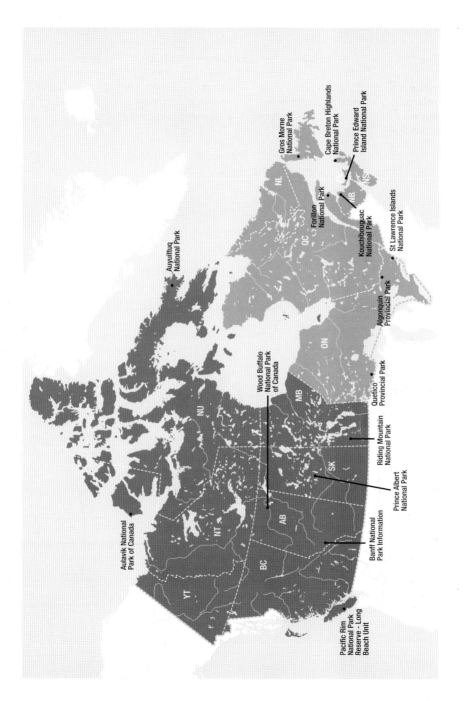

Gros Morne
National Park

Cape Breton Highlands
National Park

Prince Edward
Island National Park

Forillon
National Park

Kouchibouguac
National Park

St Lawrence Islands
National Park

Auyuittuq
National Park

Algonquin
Provincial Park

Wood Buffalo
National Park
of Canada

Quetico
Provincial Park

Riding Mountain
National Park

Prince Albert
National Park

Banff National
Park Information

Aulavik National
Park of Canada

Pacific Rim
National Park
Reserve - Long
Beach Unit

NL

QC

ON

NU

MB

SK

AB

NT

BC

YT

NB

NS

When to Go

Timing can be the most problematic aspect of a camping trip. What with weekend obligations, conflicting work and school vacations, and the general press of life's complexities, you may never seem to have the time. WRONG! If you truly want to go camping, you really can make the time—maybe not for a month-long trek in the Himalayas, but certainly enough to experience a change of routine and enjoy nature.

TRIP DURATION

The first misconception to overcome is the notion that every camping trip has to be *impressive*. A two-day/one-night trip can be enjoyable and sufficient to recharge your spiritual batteries and can be arranged almost any weekend. The lawn can wait!

In fact, for beginners, shorter trips are better. They require less planning, less specialized equipment, and they allow you to ease into the sport, learning little bits of technique at a time. Especially for families with young children, a two-day car-camping trip with one night in a tent in a state park can be a real adventure. Stretch it to include a Friday takeoff and an extra night out and it's a veritable expedition for a six-year-old.

Going Long

As worthwhile as weekend trips may be, longer ones can be even more desirable. Many campers feel that it takes three or four days before the habits and patterns of civilization begin to dissipate and they get into a "wilderness rhythm." Then take another three or four days to revel in that newfound camper's consciousness before it's time to readjust, plan your exit, and rejoin the civilized world.

Many goal-oriented camping trips require the scheduling of an extended block of time away from work. If you want to canoe 100 miles down a river, hike a small mountain chain, or take a 300-mile bicycle tour through a historic region with stops for sightseeing, you might need a week or so. If kids are in the picture, plan your time off to coincide with a school vacation.

Don't forget travel time to and from the camping area. If it takes you the better part of a day to drive each way, then a nine-day trip (two weekends plus the intervening work week) gives you one week of camping time. It's also a good idea to allow yourself a full day at the end of a trip to clean, dry, and put away your gear, rest weary muscles, and prepare to reenter the working world. (Remember that lawn?) That brings the time actually spent camping down to six days.

Seasonality and Weather

Beginning campers should plan their first trips when fair weather can be expected. Cold-weather camping requires special skills and equipment; extreme hot weather poses health dangers and logistical problems (like where can you refill your water containers?); and persistent rain simply makes things less pleasant and more difficult. With some experience, all of these concerns recede in importance. But if setting up a tent and cooking on a camp stove represent new experiences, try to keep weather-related challenges to a minimum.

By all means keep track of the weather report before you go, but do *not* cancel a trip simply because rain is predicted. (Hurricane? Yes. Showers? No way!) How often do the forecasts prove wrong? Far too many camping trips are aborted because of the mere threat of rain when the weekend in fact turns out fine.

In most regions, you simply have to count on at least some rain on trips of a week or more. If you're prepared, it's just a passing inconvenience—or maybe a good excuse to spend a day relaxing in the tent, reading and playing cards.

On a two-day trip, however, a persistent rainstorm is enough to ruin most people's camping experience. If you've already made camp when the rain arrives, you might want to stick it out and hope for the best. But camping is supposed to be fun, and it's okay to bail out if the weather gods are against you.

All this assumes that you'll be sleeping in a tent. RVers can tolerate worse weather because their vehicles are relatively snug and self-contained.

↗
Cold-weather camping requires special skills and equipment, and careful planning.

Meal Planning

The food you eat when camping may be identical to what you eat at home, or it might differ greatly, depending upon how you travel and how long you'll be out. Careful meal planning is essential to self-powered campers, who are limited in the amounts of food and cookware they can carry, but who require an unusual amount of calories to sustain their physical exertion.

FRESH FOODS

Fresh meats, dairy products, fruits, and vegetables are unquestionably more appealing than their alternatives. Unfortunately, they require refrigeration and, unless you're camping in the dead of winter, this means a refrigerator in an RV, or an ice chest in a canoe or car. In anything short of desert heat, a large ice chest of good quality will keep food fresh for four to six days if properly stocked with block (not cube) ice.

Except in very hot weather, backpackers and bike campers can safely bring some perishables for the first night out. One trick is to freeze the meat solid and use it as an ice block to keep other perishables cool. Beyond Day One, fresh foods should be limited to a few durable fruits and veggies like onions, potatoes, cabbage, and oranges, and even these won't last long if it's warm. Cheese is the only dairy product that will last more than a day without refrigeration, and that is only if it's wrapped in wax or vacuum-sealed in plastic packaging.

JUST ADD WATER

Even these limited fresh foods may prove impractical to hikers and cyclists, however, because they are heavy. All fresh foods contain a high proportion of water, and water weighs a lot: 8.3 pounds per gallon. The same goes for food in cans and jars except that, in addition to containing lots of water, the containers themselves are heavy too.

Instead of carrying water around inside the food, bring dried foods that can be made palatable by adding water. How does this save weight? Because you carry only one or two day's worth of water at any time—not enough to rehydrate a week's worth of food. This makes water resupply an essential strategy of camping, which we'll address on pages 96–99.

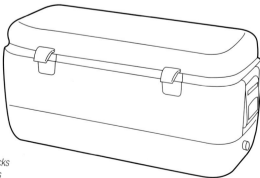

↗
Stock a cooler with blocks of ice rather than cubes

↗ *Freeze-dried meals come in packets.*

Highly nutritional foods that are light in weight and low in moisture include pasta, grains (e.g., rice, bulgur, quinoa, buckwheat), dried beans and lentils, dried or smoked meats (e.g., jerky, hard salami), and dried fruits and vegetables. Also consider the freeze-dried meals made especially for hikers.

AVOID HIGH-VOLUME FOODS

Hikers, bikers, and boat campers should avoid foods like chips, packaged breakfast cereals, and marshmallows that take up more than their fair share of pack volume for the amount of nutrition they provide. Good alternatives are gorp (a.k.a. trail mix), dense, non crushable cereals like granola and muesli, and hard candies or energy bars. Fresh eggs, though dense in protein and moderately resistant to spoilage, require so much padding that they become highly volume-inefficient.

THE RESUPPLY OPTION

Considerations of weight and volume may be moderated by the expedient of resupply. Depending upon the nature of your camping trip—essentially, whether you're within easy reach of a store or not—it may not be necessary to carry your entire menu in your pack. Planned resupply gives you flexibility and makes fresh food more practical.

Calories—Lots of Them

A day of vigorous hiking or cycling can require two to three times as many calories as a day at the office. The good news is that you can eat all you want. The bad news is that you have to carry two or three times as much food as you're accustomed to eating, per day. Carbohydrates give up their calories most readily, while fats are hard to digest. Plan your daily menus to provide roughly 60 percent of your calories from complex carbohydrates, 20 percent from proteins, and 20 percent from fats.

What's to Eat?

Consider these factors when menu planning:

- ☐ **Weight:** Include packaging.
- ☐ **Volume:** Does it take up too much space for the amount of nutrition it provides?
- ☐ **Durability and perishability:** Will it go bad? get crushed? melt? Does it need refrigeration?
- ☐ **Taste:** If you hate it at home, will you like it in the field?
- ☐ **Variety:** Do you really want to eat it five meals in a row?
- ☐ **Nutritional content:** Vigorous exercise burns a lot of calories that must be replenished. Also consider protein, vitamins, and minerals.
- ☐ **Preparation:** Does it require water or special cookware? Can you prepare it over a campstove or fire? Is it quick and easy? Most backcountry campers prefer one-pot meals to simplify preparation and wash-up, minimize fuel use, and limit cooking to a single stove.

Camping in Other Countries

It's a wide world, lending even greater diversity to camping overseas. In most first-world countries, you can pursue the same types of camping as in the U.S., from backpacking the backwoods to RVing near theme parks. In developing countries, accurate maps may be nonexistent and you might be unable to find familiar foods or fuel for your stove. But the benefits are natural sights you'll never see at home, and exposure to new cultures.

OUTFITTERS

Unless you're an experienced camper, don't try to arrange your own foreign camping trip. There's too much to learn about camping right at home for you to want to complicate it with foreign languages, laws, cuisine, and customs.

If you're determined to take your first camping trip overseas, use an outfitter that specializes in your country of interest. These companies know how to plan a successful trip, and they've worked out the logistics and legal formalities. You show up at the airport with your personal gear and they take over, guiding you over trails they know to huts or campsites they've used before. You're virtually assured of experiencing the kind of natural beauty and cultural contact you had in mind.

Foreign Camping Considerations

- ☐ **Passport:** Make sure yours is current.
- ☐ **Visa:** Find out if your destination country requires one, and if it must be obtained prior to arrival.
- ☐ **Other paperwork:** Some countries require special hiking or camping permits or proofs of vaccinations.
- ☐ **Currency:** Check with your local bank. Changing dollars for the local currency at the arrival airport is usually the worst place to do it if you want a favorable exchange rate.
- ☐ **Credit card:** Some banks charge oppressive fees for purchases made in other currencies; others are more reasonable.
- ☐ **Drugs:** Take what you need with you, and carry a copy of your prescription for legal protection.
- ☐ **Health:** Check with the U.S. Department of State for health warnings concerning the country you will visit and get the appropriate vaccinations or prophylactics.
- ☐ **Stove and fuel:** Stove fuels cannot travel by air. Find out if the fuel you need is available at your destination, and ask the airline how to prepare your stove so that it can be packed in your luggage.
- ☐ **Backpack:** Airlines don't treat packs well. Secure all straps, or remove them and pack them inside. Better yet, place the whole pack in a large duffel or encase it in industrial stretch-wrap and strapping tape.
- ☐ **Maps and trail guides:** Especially in developing countries, you can't count on finding these after you arrive. Do your research and obtain materials before leaving home.
- ☐ **Language:** The more of the local language you know, the better. Make it a point to learn at least the basic "politeness" phrases: hello, please, yes, no, I'm sorry, I don't speak (the language), where's the restroom? "Help" is another good one.
- ☐ **Culture:** Learn about the local culture before you leave home. You'll avoid *faux pas* and potentially dangerous misunderstandings, and you'll gain a deeper appreciation for what you encounter.

Planning

Gear

Techniques

Hazards

Hiking

Camping with Kids

Fitness and Health

Many camping trips are interrupted on their second day by sore muscles. Unless you hike, bike, or paddle on a regular basis, these activities will subject your body to unaccustomed stresses. Even RV camping may involve an unusual level of physical activity for some couch potatoes. Better get in shape before you start.

HOW'S YOUR HEALTH?

Many beginners are attracted to camping by stories of impressive feats like hiking the Adirondack Trail or biking across the country, yet some of these same beginners won't willingly walk across a Walmart parking lot or bike two miles to pick up some milk.

Be realistic about your abilities and your inclinations. The first thing you can do is get active. Walk or bike instead of drive. Take the stairs. Carry your bags instead of rolling them.

Before setting out on a trip that's at all physically demanding, see your physician for a physical checkup. Make sure your cardiovascular health is up to it. Get treatment for that painful knee.

TRAINING

Cycling places unusual demands on your heart, lungs, and legs, and backpacking demands all that plus a strong back. Canoeing and kayaking require good arm, shoulder, and upper-body strength and mobility and, if any *portaging* (carrying the canoe) is involved, a strong back and legs as well.

The best way to begin improving all of these physical capabilities is to start engaging in the sport in a modest way. Take day hikes with a light pack. Ride your bike without luggage, or go paddling for a couple hours. Gradually increase the duration and the load until you're confident you can do it day after day in the field with your full camping burden. The pre-camping runs will also help break in your boots, toughen your feet, hands, and butt, and reveal any weaknesses in your equipment.

Busy schedules often prohibit daily hikes and canoeing, but workouts at home or at the gym can make up the difference and help prevent injury. Build up your arm, leg, and back muscles with weight training. Use a treadmill, stationary bike, or similar equipment to boost your cardiovascular health. Do stretches and mobility exercises to reduce the chance of sprains.

BE PREPARED FOR EMERGENCIES

Whether or not it's been documented scientifically, it is likely that a study would find that accidents occur more frequently when camping than at other times. This is mainly due to the unusual physical demands of the activities, but also partly to the use of unfamiliar equipment like axes, camping stoves, and folding knives.

It's essential to be prepared to deal with medical emergencies—not only because of their frequency, but also because of your probable remoteness from professional medical attention when they occur. Learn first-aid and bring a first-aid kit on every camping trip. (See pages 62–64 and 128–132.)

The Ethics of Camping

Like nearly every other human activity, camping has standards of ethics. They exist to protect the environment and to maximize the enjoyment of the wilderness for all users. Even in the most remote campsite, your actions will ultimately affect others. This chapter is simply an overview of camping ethics to get you in the right frame of mind: ethical behavior and the principle of minimal impact underlie all the procedures described elsewhere.

MINIMIZE IMPACTS

"Minimal impact" is the rule of thumb for wilderness ethics. In other words, do as little to disturb the environment *and other campers* as possible. So-called "leave-no-trace" camping is a particularly rigorous application of this regime.

Most popular camping and wilderness areas already exhibit substantial human impact. Hiking and biking trails eliminate ground cover and cut a path through vegetation. Campsites do the same, especially where tents are pitched and in areas set aside for cooking and eating. Fire rings and trash accumulation can disfigure the area, and firewood is often denuded in a large circle around established campsites.

As unattractive as these impacts may be, there's a good side to it. Heavy usage in a limited, defined area means little or no impact across surrounding areas. By concentrating impacts, we spare the larger environment.

Protecting the Environment

Some of the ways in which campers can disturb—or avoid disturbing—the environment include:

Tent location: Don't place your tent on fresh vegetation. Use established sites that are already bare.

Fires: Secure fire permits when required, and abide by fire restrictions if in effect. Exhibit scrupulous care to avoid setting forest fires. Keep fires small: build them only large enough to do the job at hand.

Fire rings: Use existing fire rings, and don't build new ones. If they contain others' trash, pack it out. If a fire ring contains charred wood, burn it in your own fire.

Firewood: Burn only down wood. Cut no live trees or even standing dead wood.

Washing: Clean plates and cookware so as to avoid leaving food scraps for scavengers. When washing dishes or your body, avoid contaminating water sources with soap.

Wildlife: Avoid disturbing wildlife. View only from a distance. Never feed or otherwise intentionally attract animals. Secure food against scavengers.

Vegetation: Avoid walking on, removing, or otherwise damaging living plants.

Trails: Stay on established or marked trails, even if they are wet or muddy, to avoid creating new ruts and trampling otherwise untouched plants.

Interpersonal Ethics

In addition to protecting the environment, camping ethics exist to protect the rights of other campers. Observe the following considerations when camping:

Group size: Hike in groups of no more than six. If there are more people in your party, split up into smaller groups and meet at a prearranged campsite.

Quiet: Keep the noise level to a minimum at all times. Quiet maximizes your chances of seeing wildlife and avoids disturbing other campers who may wish to enjoy the sounds of nature or simply get some sleep. Know this: *everyone* hates someone else's radio when camping.

Planning

Gear

Techniques

Hazards

Hiking

Camping with Kids

Human waste/sanitary paper goods:
Dispose of it properly, so that it is neither visible nor "smellable," cannot be stepped on, and cannot pollute water sources. Burial of feces is acceptable in some areas; in others it must be packed out.

Garbage: Burn it to ash or pack it out. No exceptions.

Alcohol and illicit drugs: See "Quiet," on the previous page.

Dogs: Observe restrictions. Keep dogs under control and on a leash at all times. Do not allow them to disturb wildlife or other campers. If your dog is a barker, don't bring it.

Campsite courtesy: In areas where camping is restricted to established campsites, make room for groups who have nowhere else to go. Keep your gear neat and contained. Be friendly and helpful, but observe others' wishes for privacy.

Trail courtesy: Make way for others who wish to pass in either direction. See "Quiet," on the previous page.

Gear and provisions: Bring what you need for comfort and safety. Be willing to share with another camper in need.

Safety: Consider your group to be on its own, responsible for its own safety. Avoid situations that might call for others to bail you out of difficulties. Nonetheless, leave a "flight plan" with a trusted friend so that others can find you if you go missing. Provide help when it's needed if you can do so without endangering yourself.

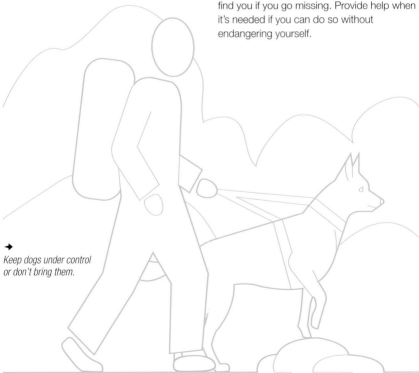

➜
*Keep dogs under control
or don't bring them.*

Gathering Information

Information is the start of every successful camping trip. You can't prepare until you know where you're going and what it's like. From terrain to campsite availability to permit requirements, you need to nail down the details before you go.

LOCAL RESOURCES

Especially if your first trips will be close to home, information is probably available from local sources. Most of the people who work at privately owned outfitters are there because they know and love camping, and they'll be glad to provide information on good trips nearby—especially if you need to buy equipment.

Join a local or state camping, bicycling, or paddling club. They are great sources of expertise, and most run frequent organized trips, so you can have your first experiences in company with folks who already have the technical skills and know the best local sites. The same goes for local or state chapters of national organizations like the Sierra Club and the Audubon Society, or large regional groups like the Appalachian Mountain Club in the Northeast and The Mountaineers in the Northwest.

GOVERNMENT AGENCIES

The government agencies that run large chunks of land are the best source for certain types of information—but not all. If you want to camp in a state or national park, then the agency in charge is certainly the place to go to ask about reservations and rules. Their

websites vary in accuracy and detail, but at least you can find contact information for someone to call or email.

The main offices of the large agencies often don't have detailed information about specific properties under their control. You can't expect someone in Washington, DC, to know about trail conditions this year at a park in Colorado. For that, you need to talk to a ranger at that park.

However, even the local rangers can't possibly have first-hand experience of every corner of a 500,000-acre wilderness; that's where the experience of local campers and outfitters comes back into the picture. Ask around, and someone's almost certain to have done it before. Furthermore, government employees may be prohibited from offering personal advice. So if the question is something like "do you think I'll enjoy this trip?", you might get a more useful answer from a local outfitter or club member.

RESEARCH RESOURCES

Almost every popular camping location is covered by one or more guidebooks or trail guides. Most are updated frequently to accommodate changes in rules, trails, and resources, so avoid old editions.

Internet resources are endless, not only to research camping destinations, but for technical know-how as well. Here are a few good ones to get you started:

Loyalty Pays Off

If you rely on a local vendor for information, don't turn around and buy your gear online. The little extra you might pay locally is what makes that source of expertise possible.

What Info?

Planning a camping trip requires gathering a lot of information. Here are the important issues. Not every item will apply to every trip.

General Trip Data
☐ Driving directions
☐ Climate
☐ Social/cultural background (if foreign)
☐ Local/regional history

Campgrounds
☐ Fees
☐ Reservations
☐ Check-in/check-out time
☐ Minimum/maximum length of stay
☐ Size of campsite: will it accommodate your RV or the number of people and tents you have?
☐ Hookups: electric, internet, water
☐ Dump site
☐ Amenities (store, activities, swimming, etc.)

Hiking Trails and Backcountry Sites
☐ Get trail maps, topographic maps, trail guides
☐ What are the terrain/roads/river conditions?
☐ How are trails marked?
☐ Alternate routes/bail-out points if you need to cut the trip short
☐ Are camping permits and/or check-in/check-out required?
☐ Where are established campsites? How are they marked?
☐ Is camping permitted outside of established campsites?
☐ Are fires permitted? Are fire permits required?
☐ Water sources: location and potability
☐ Rules for human waste disposal
☐ Local dangers or hazards
☐ Contacts and protocols for emergencies

Recreation.gov: An amazing location and activity finder for federal nature and outdoor recreation facilities. Pick a general or specific location, specify a desired activity (e.g., RV camping, fishing, etc.) and it'll show you where to go on an interactive map. Click the map for details and links to the web page for any facility.

Reserve America (www.reserveamerica. com): A centralized booking engine for most federal and many state and private campgrounds and campsites. Incorporates the National Recreation Reservation System. Invaluable for the most popular national parks.

GORP (www.gorp.com): Articles about places to camp, gear reviews, how-to, and a nice park finder. Geared toward the human-powered camper.

Woodall's (www.woodalls.com): Similar to GORP but intended specifically for RVs and car campers.

U.S. Geological Survey (www.usgs.gov): Topographic maps covering the entire United States can be ordered on paper or downloaded free. Also sells maps of U.S. Forest Service and National Park facilities.

2 GEAR

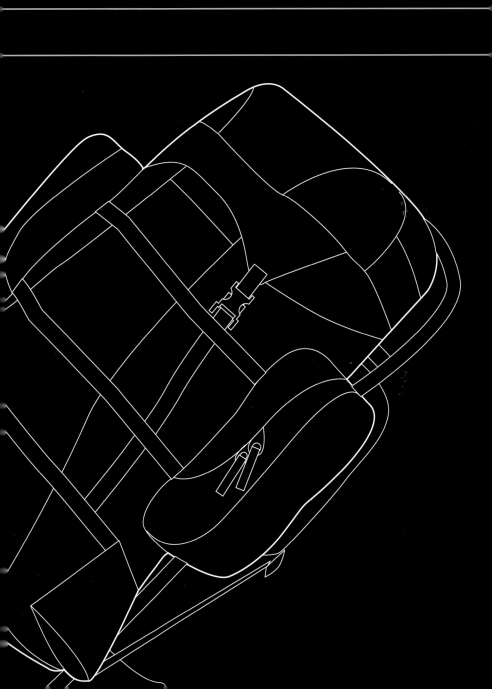

Tents

Tents are impressive examples of fabric engineering: light and small enough to be carried easily, yet strong enough to resist high winds, waterproof in a downpour, and large enough when assembled to house you and your gear. No wonder they're often the most expensive piece of gear in a camper's closet. There is a huge number of variables in tent design, making it somewhat of a challenge to choose one that suits your needs.

1 *Dome tent*

TYPES OF TENTS

Among the many different configurations available, four are by far the most popular and best suited to most campers:

1. Dome Tents
Roughly hemispherical in shape. The curved poles that cross each other make dome tents self-supporting (also known as freestanding): i.e., they can stand up without stakes.

2. A-Frame Tents
These have a triangular cross-section. Lighter and often much less expensive than dome tents, they have less usable interior room

because of the steeply sloping sides. Not self-supporting.

3. Tunnel or Hoop Tents
Roughly vault-shaped (i.e., half-cylinders), although many have a pronounced slope down from front to back. Not self-supporting.

4. Cabin Tents
These have tall, nearly vertical sides, a roof with a shallow pitch, and standing headroom. Spacious but heavy, they are best suited for family car-camping. Most are self-supporting.

Planning

Gear

Techniques

Hazards

Hiking

Camping with Kids

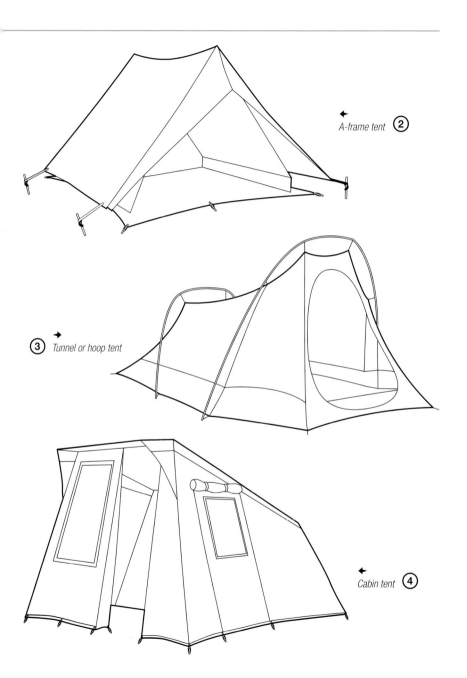

A-frame tent ②

③ Tunnel or hoop tent

Cabin tent ④

Three- or Four-Season

Tents are also categorized as either three-season or four-season based on their suitability for winter camping. Four-season tents are stronger to resist the weight of snow, and they have less mesh in their walls to reduce ventilation and maintain warmth. Cabin tents are generally not suitable for winter camping. Their tall, flat sides do not shed wind easily, and their flat "roofs," consisting of large, unsupported spans of fabric, can collapse under an accumulation of snow.

Single- or Double-Wall

Finally, tents have either single-wall or double-wall construction. In a double-wall tent, much of the sides and top of the main tent "body" are made of mesh, which keeps out bugs but also does nothing to keep out rain. A waterproof fly is placed over the tent body to keep things dry, creating a second, outer wall, with several inches of space between them. Single-wall tents have no fly: the entire tent body is made from waterproof fabric.

The double-wall design permits good ventilation, which reduces condensation of the moisture from campers' sweat and exhalation inside the tent. This is a more important consideration than it might seem, because each camper exhales about a quart of water each night! If you don't vent that moisture to the outside, it can end up dripping onto your sleeping bag.

Single-wall tents, which rely on vents for air circulation, are generally not as effective at combating condensation as double-wall tents. They are favored mainly by campers who want a tent of the lightest weight possible, and who are willing to put up with a damper interior.

Tent Alternatives

There are other ways to keep the rain off beside tents:

Tarp: A tarp can provide protection from rain or sun for cooking, eating, and other activities that you don't want to do inside the tent. The common blue polyester utility tarps suffice for car camping, but they're too heavy and bulky for backpacking or bike camping. Lightweight coated nylon and polyester tarps are available in rectangular shapes, which can be pitched in a wide variety of configurations, and in parabolic cuts, which are more stable in high winds. (See catenary-cut tarp and rectangular tarp.)

Bivy sack: A *bivy* (short for bivouac) is a waterproof bag and hood into which you slip your sleeping bag and then yourself. Often used by bicyclists to save weight, and by mountaineers as a backup shelter when they can't make it back to camp before darkness or bad weather arrives, they're a minimal shelter that provides no room for anything except sleep.

Jungle hammock: A jungle hammock has a solid fabric base and shallow mosquito-mesh sidewalls, to the top of which is sewn a waterproof tarp "roof." Favored by jungle fighters who travel light and quick, they're useful to keep you off the ground in mangrove swamps or marshy woods, away from snakes and other nasty crawlies.

Pickup bed tent: A dome tent designed to set up in the cargo bed of a full-size pickup truck, a bed tent creates a kind of cross between car-camping and RVing.

Catenary-cut tarps, which are sewn along the bias (diagonally), are more stable in a breeze.

A rectangular tarp can be pitched between two trees or a pair of sticks or trekking poles driven into the ground.

Some bivies have a hoop frame to keep the fabric off your face and a fine mesh to keep insects out.

mesh

tarp

hammock

A jungle hammock takes some getting used to, but will keep you off wet ground and away from crawling insects.

HOW BIG?

Tents are sized by the number of people they can sleep. But manufacturers' descriptions of this sort are invariably misleading. A four-person tent is really big enough to sleep three adults comfortably. Yes, you could fit four in there, but it will be crowded, and there will be no room for gear. The only exception is one-man tents, which obviously have to be big enough to hold one. My advice: unless weight is the primary concern, always buy a tent rated for at least one more person than you expect to sleep in it.

A more refined way to compare tent size is by looking at their dimensions. More floor space is usually a good thing, although larger tents naturally tend to weigh more. Compare both total floor space, and the width and length dimensions independently. Taller campers might want their square-footage laid out differently than short, husky ones. The tent must be substantially longer than you are tall, to accommodate the length of your sleeping bag beyond your feet, plus some room for gear and moving around.

Don't ignore headroom. A tent is far more livable if you can sit up comfortably. Only the largest domes (for eight or more people) and most cabin tents allow you to stand upright.

Packed Size and Weight

Another important tent dimension for backpackers and bike campers is the packed size: how big it is when it's packed in its carry sack. The length of the package is usually determined by the length of the disassembled poles, and you must be able to carry the tent in such a way as to protect the poles from damage. This is sometimes a problem for bicycle campers, who often remove the poles from the sack and strap them to their bike's rear carrier instead.

Weight is also of great importance to hikers and bikers. When comparing tents for weight, make sure you compare "apples to apples." Most manufacturers include only the tent body, poles, and fly in their "minimum" weight specification, while "total" weight also includes the stakes and carry sack. But not all tent makers abide by these standards.

QUALITY AND DURABILITY

Nylon and polyester are common tent fabrics, and both are fairly light, durable, and waterproof when coated with polyurethane or silicone. Fabric weight is measured in denier, with thicker fabrics of 70-denier (70D) being heavier and more durable than lighter ones of 30D or 40D.

Aluminum poles, which are found on most better, more expensive tents, are lighter in weight and less prone to breakage than fiberglass ones.

Except for ultralight tents that omit the floor altogether, all better tents have a "bathtub"-style floor, in which the floor material curves a few inches up the sides to minimize seams at ground level. Only the cheapest tents have blue polytarp-like material for floors: these are not very durable, and should be avoided unless cost is an overriding concern.

Tent Features

Unless you're embarking on a serious expedition, you don't need every available premium feature. But here are some to consider:

Windows and vents: How many windows and vents, and how large are they?

Footprint: A ground cloth made to fit the size and shape of the tent.

Tie-backs: To secure doors, windows, and screens when they're open.

Second entrance: Depending on the tent's layout, a second "door" may be helpful to avoid waking your partner when you have to take a midnight run to the bathroom.

Vestibule or porch: Covered, floorless space in front of the door that allows you to store gear out of the rain while avoiding bringing mud and rain into the main body of the tent.

Body-to-pole attachment: On some tents, the poles slip through sleeves in the fabric. On others, clips that are sewn to the fabric attach to the poles. Clips are easier to use; sleeves are stronger. Most good-quality backpacking tents now use clips, and sleeves are generally reserved for only the cheapest tents and the most rugged four-season tents.

Mesh pockets: Sewn to the inside of the tent, these are handy for stashing your flashlight and eyeglasses at night.

Gear loft: A fabric shelf near the roof of the tent to hold lightweight items.

Flashlight loop: A fabric loop sewn into the roof from which a small flashlight or lantern can be suspended.

Fly-only pitch: In mosquito-free areas, some ultralight campers skip the tent body and use only the fly and a ground cloth. Not all tent designs will accommodate this arrangement.

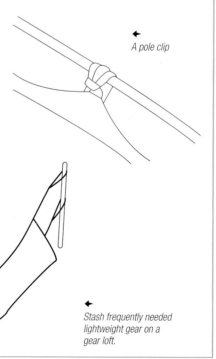

← *A pole clip*

← *Stash frequently needed lightweight gear on a gear loft.*

Planning

Gear

Techniques

Hazards

Hiking

Camping with Kids

Sleeping Bags and Pads

At home, if your blanket doesn't keep you warm, you just throw on another, or turn up the thermostat. In camp, a good night's sleep depends upon a good sleeping bag that will keep you warm enough, but not too warm. The other half of the sleep equation is a pad to place between the bag and the floor of the tent.

TEMPERATURE RATINGS

Sleeping bags are rated by temperature. You'll see 40 degree bags, 20 degree bags, even –20 degree bags (all Fahrenheit in the U.S.). These numbers indicate the minimum temperature at which the bag is supposed to keep you comfortable. But these are rough guidelines, and no industry standard exists, so one manufacturer's 30 degree bag could be equivalent to another's 40 degree bag.

Also, of course, everyone has a different sense of what's a comfortable sleeping temperature. If you're a "hot" sleeper, matching the degree rating with the coldest temperature you expect to encounter might work out well. If you sleep "cold," choose a bag rated at least 10 degrees lower than the coldest temperatures you expect to camp in.

If your bag is too warm, you can always open it up. Making it warmer, though, isn't so easy. If you plan to camp throughout the year in a wide range of temperatures, you will probably need more than one sleeping bag.

SHAPE AND SIZE

Mummy bags are shaped to fit the body closely. They weigh the least of any sleeping bag shape, pack smallest, and keep you warmest, because there's less empty space inside for your body to keep warm. The downside is that you can't readily turn around inside them: when you roll over, the bag rolls with you.

Car campers often choose rectangular sleeping bags, which are heavier, not as warm, but more spacious. Although there are some excellent rectangular bags, almost all of the cheapest bags are rectangular. Many RVers use rectangular bags unzipped to open flat like a comforter.

Between mummies and rectangulars are tapered bags, also known as semi-mummies or semi-rectangulars. As you'd expect, they tend to split the difference in terms of weight, warmth, and spaciousness.

All mummies and most semi-mummies have insulated hoods that cover your head but leave your face exposed. People lose a great deal of body heat through the head, so keeping your head warm is key to keeping warm overall. If your sleeping bag lacks a hood, wear a warm cap in cold weather.

Buy a bag to suit your size. A "tall" bag made for a camper over six feet leaves a lot of unused space at the bottom if you're 5'4". That empty space is hard to keep warm, and it represents weight that you'd probably rather not carry.

MATERIALS

Sleeping bags are filled either with goose down or synthetic fibers. Down is warmer, lighter, and packs more compactly than synthetics. It's also more expensive; it loses virtually all of its insulating properties if it gets wet; and it's difficult to dry.

Good-quality sleeping bags with synthetic filling use proprietary fibers such as Hollofil, Quallofil, or Polarguard. While these are all available in various grades, they are far superior in terms of warmth-per-weight to the no-name polyester batting in the cheapest bags. Synthetic-filled bags retain at least some of their insulating properties when wet, and they dry more quickly than down, so they are strongly favored by boat campers.

The fabric shell of most bags is either nylon or polyester: there isn't a great deal of performance difference between them. Some bags have a waterproof coating on the outer fabric.

Sleeping Bag Options

Stuff sacks: Virtually all sleeping bags come with carrying bags known as stuff sacks. Waterproof versions are available from camping specialty retailers. Another option is the compression sack: a stuff sack with buckles and straps sewn on that allows you to crush the bag down an extra 30 percent or so to save room in your pack.

Bag liners: A light fabric bag placed inside the sleeping bag helps keep the sleeping bag clean and adds 10°F or more extra warmth.

Double bags: Double-width bags allow couples to sleep together.

Zip-together bags: These are two bags of identical design and construction but with mirror-image configuration and matching zippers, to make a double bag when desired and serve as solo bags the rest of the time.

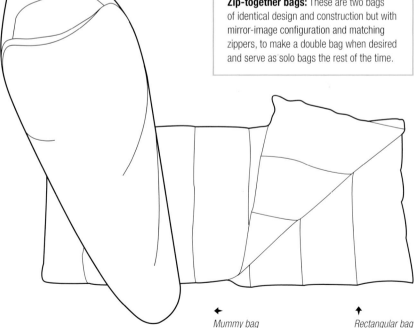

← *Mummy bag*   ↑ *Rectangular bag*

Planning

Gear

Techniques

Hazards

Hiking

Camping with Kids

Sleeping Bag Care

Down bags pack more compactly if they are stuffed into the stuff sack and not rolled up. It is also believed that stuffing prevents the down from being permanently compressed and losing its insulating properties. Synthetic bags may be either rolled or stuffed.

Sleeping bags should only be transported in their stuff sacks, never stored in them. Keeping the bag in the sack will compress the insulation permanently. When you arrive in camp, pull the bag out of its sack and lay it flat as soon as your tent is set up to give the insulation a chance to rebound. At home, hang the bag on a hanger or store it loosely in a large plastic trash bag.

Minimize the need for washing a sleeping bag by using a bag liner and avoiding spills. If washing is necessary, follow the

manufacturer's instructions, which generally call for hand-washing with mild soap. Never dry-clean a sleeping bag.

PADS AND SUCH

The insulation in your sleeping bag compresses beneath your weight as you sleep so that it does little to protect you from the cold, hard ground. That's why, for tent campers, a pad is a virtual necessity.

The traditional low-cost option is a roll of dense, closed-cell foam, but many campers now opt for self-inflating pads, which are more comfortable and generally less bulky. These have compressible foam inside an airtight envelope. For transport, the pad is rolled up tight, and much of the air is forced out through a valve. When you're ready to make up your bed, you open the valve, air enters the envelope, and the foam expands. Close the valve and lie down. In the morning, open the valve and roll up the pad, forcing the air out again.

Self-inflating pads are only an inch or two thick—just enough to cushion you from the ground. Some campers prefer the traditional multi-chambered air mattress, which provides more cushioning but little thermal insulation. Car campers can take this a step further and use a full-fledged inflatable mattress of the type used for overnight guests at home. For car-campers who'd like something more like a conventional bed, a final option is the folding camp-cot.

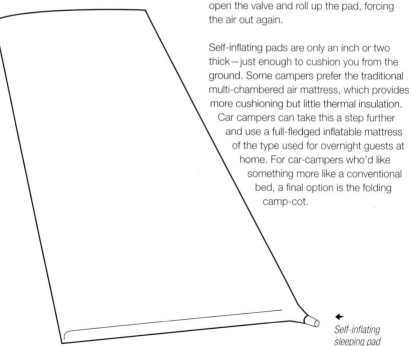

←
*Self-inflating
sleeping pad*

Clothing

Clothing dominates most camping gear catalogs and websites, which betray a strong fashion-industry influence, playing up the notion that being well-dressed for camping means looking good. Go for it if you're so inclined, but be comforted, if you will, that camping doesn't have to be a fashion contest. Here we'll consider only the practical side of being "well-dressed," and we'll focus on clothes appropriate for all campers, and especially backpackers. Bicyclists and canoeists will additionally want to look into speciality clothing appropriate for their sports.

THE LAYERING PRINCIPLE

Your camping wardrobe has a difficult job to do. It must keep you warm in cold weather and keep you cool when it's hot. It has to be rugged, but light weight is a virtue. Most difficult and possibly most important, it must keep you dry.

Staying dry is difficult because hard work—like hiking—makes you sweat. Cover yourself with raingear and you'll sweat even harder, so even though you might keep off the rain, you'll still get wet. Getting wet quickly leads to getting cold, the consequences of which can range from uncomfortable to deadly.

The solution to this conundrum is layering—dressing in three layers designed to keep you warm and dry.

The Inner Layer

The inner or base layer is what you wear against your skin—underwear, if you will. The purpose of the base layer is to move moisture in the form of sweat away from your skin by either absorbing it or by capillary action (i.e., *wicking*) to the next layer. In anything but T-shirt weather, you should wear a base layer and an outer layer on your torso. As the weather gets cooler, you should add a base layer to your bottom half as well. Good materials for base layers are polypropylene, polyester, and silk.

Base Layer Materials

Fiber	Pros	Cons
Wool	• Absorbs lots of moisture	• Dries slowly • Itchy • Bulky
Silk	• Absorbs lots of moisture • Feels wonderful • Lightweight	• Difficult to clean • Dries slowly • Expensive
Polypropylene	• Wicks moisture effectively • Dries quickly	• Some retain odors • Some are difficult to clean • Some are scratchy
Polyester	• Wicks moisture effectively • Dries quickly • Washes easily	• No significant problems

Planning

Gear

Techniques

Hazards

Hiking

Camping with Kids

The Middle Layer

Above the base layer is the middle layer—sometimes confusingly called the outer layer. A better term for it might be the *insulating* layer, for that is its function. The middle layer creates an envelope of dead air around your body, which is warmed by your body's own heat and that, in turn, warms you back.

A heavy wool shirt or sweater is the traditional middle layer: both are thick so they hold a lot of air, and wool will readily absorb moisture passed to it from the base layer. Popular modern choices are polyester or nylon fleece or pile, which trap air and wick moisture to their outer surface where it can evaporate.

The Shell

This is the real outer layer, but we won't call it that, to avoid confusing it with the middle "outer" layer. The shell serves as a windbreaker, to prevent that envelope of warm, dead air in the middle layer from being blown away and replaced by cold air. It also provides protection against rain.

Wearing vinyl raingear is like placing yourself in a plastic bag. It'll protect you from the rain, but you'll poach from inside. Coated nylon and polyester fabrics are somewhat better, and well-made outerwear of these fabrics may include clever venting systems to expel moisture. The gold standard for rainproof shells is Gore-Tex and similar fabrics that contain a microporous membrane. The pores in this membrane are too small for raindrops to enter, but large enough for water vapor to escape. It's expensive and its performance is not flawless, but most outdoors people feel it's the best available option. For full rain protection, wear rain pants of the same fabric as your jacket.

WHAT ELSE TO WEAR

The layering principle assumes bad weather. It's always a good idea to be prepared for the worst conditions, but let's look at the rest of your camping wardrobe:

Gloves: Fleece is a good choice for moderately cool weather.

Shirt: Cotton is a good cool choice for hot, dry weather. Cotton-nylon blends dry more quickly and are a better all-weather choice.

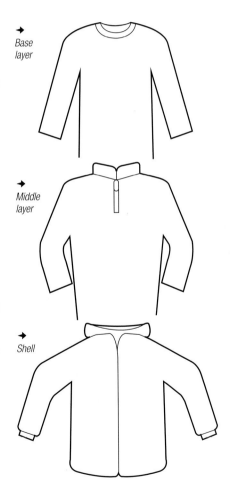

➜ *Base layer*

➜ *Middle layer*

➜ *Shell*

Trousers: Wool pants or heavy-weight nylon-spandex leggings are good choices for cool, wet conditions. All-nylon dries quickly and feels cool: it's good if you expect to get wet in warm weather. Cotton-nylon blends are warmer than all-nylon, dry moderately quickly, and are good for all-around use. Trousers that convert to shorts by unzipping the lower parts of the legs are highly recommended: you can start out long in the cool of the morning, and convert to short as the day warms up.

Hat: A warm knit or fleece cap for cool nights and mornings; a broad-brimmed hat for sun and rain.

↑
A broad-brimmed hat offers protection from sun and rain.

Ponchos

A poncho is a viable alternative to a rain jacket. Because they're open at the bottom, they vent moisture readily, so expensive Gore-Tex is unnecessary. Some backpackers' ponchos have an extra-long tail, to fit over the backpack and keep it dry too. If equipped with grommets around the edges, a large poncho can be used as a tarp for an emergency shelter. But ponchos flap in the wind, and some campers are uncomfortable with an overgarment that lacks sleeves.

Bandanas

A large cotton bandana is a valuable multifunctional accessory. Tie it around your neck to absorb sweat and avoid sunburn. Dip it in water and tie it around your head or neck to keep cool. Use it as a pot holder, berry basket, bandage, sling, or even as a handkerchief.

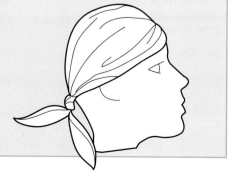

Planning

Gear

Techniques

Hazards

Hiking

Camping with Kids

Footwear

Car campers and RVers rarely need to give their feet any special attention. Whatever works during any weekend at home generally works for them when camping. Bike campers wear bicycling shoes on the road, and can change into sandals or athletic shoes in camp. But the feet of backpackers and boat campers face unusual conditions and need to be protected accordingly by wearing the right boots or shoes.

HIKING BOOTS

Good hiking boots do a lot. They provide traction on a range of surfaces, support your arches and your ankles, and protect your feet from rocks. They try to do this without creating blisters, while weighing as little as possible and lasting as long as possible.

General-purpose hiking boots come in light-, medium, and heavy-duty versions. Lighter boots make it less tiring to hike, while heavier ones provide more support and protection. Lighter boots are generally cooler, which is sometimes desirable, sometimes not. They're also more flexible, easier to break in, and less likely to produce blisters. Heavier shoes are more durable and often provide superior waterproofing.

The harder your hiking, the heavier your boots should be. If you'll be carrying a 50-pound pack and clambering through boulder fields, you'll appreciate the extra support, stiffness, and protection of a heavy boot.

Trail Shoes

An alternative to the hiking boot is the trail shoe. These are constructed like light hiking boots, but they're cut low, like running shoes. They offer no ankle support, but some hikers prefer them for their lighter weight and coolness.

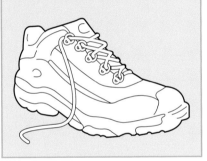

Most backpackers choose medium-weight boots as a good compromise of qualities. There are still plenty of options, for example whether the boot is insulated, whether it's waterproof, and whether the uppers are primarily fabric (cooler, quicker, drying, maintenance-free) or leather (more durable, more waterproof).

Sizing Boots

Buying hiking boots is always a bit of a gamble, because what seems comfortable in the store might not be after a few miles on the trail. But there are a few measures you can take to minimize the risk.

Hiking boot

Camp Shoes

Bring a second set of footgear to give your feet a rest at the end of a long day on the trail, and to dry your boots if necessary. Moccasins, running shoes, and sport sandals all make good camp shoes.

Try the boots on with the same socks you'll hike in. With the boot untied, push your foot forward until your toes just touch the inside of the toe box. You should then be able to push your index finger between your heel and the back of the boot without having to force it in, but with no room to spare.

Next, tie the boots comfortably tight and try to force your feet forward inside them. The ends of your toes should not come into contact with the inside of the toe box. Try to shift your foot sideways inside the shoe: there should be no movement at all.

Breaking In Boots

It's essential to break boots in before a backpacking trip. This process loosens and softens the material and molds it to the shape of your foot. Failure to break in your boots is just asking for blisters. Wear them around town or while doing yard work. Take a few day hikes: it is advisable to walk at least 25 miles in new boots before heading out on a longer, multi-day trip.

FOOTGEAR FOR BOAT CAMPERS

Boat campers need footgear that will either dry quickly or keep their feet dry. Hiking boots, trail shoes, and athletic shoes dry too slowly, but there are several other options:

Sport sandals: Comfortable in warm weather and can be worn with neoprene socks when it's cold. Some give good traction on wet rocks and good protection to your foot's sole but little protection around the uppers and no ankle support.

Neoprene paddling booties: Keep your feet warm even when wet. The soles provide good traction, but there is no ankle support.

Rubber boots: Warm but sweaty. The loose fit means they're not good for portaging or hiking, and they're potentially dangerous if you capsize, as they fill with water.

Portage boots: Built like hiking boots but drain water and dry quickly. They offer good support and traction for portaging.

SOCKS

Avoid cotton socks. They provide little warmth even when dry. When you sweat, they get wet and, if you're hiking, they'll chafe against your feet and generate blisters.

The traditional choice is to wear two socks (on each foot!): a thin liner sock of nylon, polypropylene, or some other wicking material, and a midweight or heavy wool or wool-blend outer sock for warmth and cushioning. The two-sock approach helps avoid blisters because the socks slide against each other.

The modern option is synthetic hiking socks, which have extra padding at the toe and heel, and protect well against blisters.

Both approaches work, but you may have to choose one and stick with it—at least as long as your hiking boots last—because your boots might not accommodate the different thicknesses of the different approaches.

The Kitchen

Much of the camping day revolves around cooking and eating. It's the first task in the morning, often the dominant thought when you're on the trail, the road, or the lake, and the major activity between the time you pitch your tent in the afternoon and when you enter it to sleep at night. For non-automotive campers, it's also a major logistical challenge to pack and carry all your food and everything you need to cook and eat it with.

STOVES

Despite their valuable function as a focal point for night-time activities, few campers do their cooking over campfires. Gathering firewood is often problematic; lighting a fire is a skill that many never master; and stoves are simply easier to cook over.

Stoves may be classed by those that are suitable for backpackers, which are smaller than a coffee can, and "camp" stoves, which may be briefcase-size or larger. The latter are too big for backpacking, but suitable for automotive and some boat campers. Backpacker stoves invariably have a single burner; camp stoves often have two. Beyond the issue of size and weight, stoves differ by the type of fuel they burn.

1. Liquid Fuel Stoves

Most liquid-fuel stoves burn white gas (i.e., Coleman fuel), and some will additionally work with unleaded gasoline, kerosene, jet fuel, naphtha, and/or diesel fuel. Before they can start cooking, they need to be primed by burning a small amount of fuel in an attached spirit cup, to begin vaporizing the cooking fuel. The traditional Coleman two-burner stove, as big as a small suitcase, is a well-known liquid-fuel stove. Some backpacking stoves have a built-in fuel tank, which may hold enough gas for a weekend, but most draw their fuel from an external bottle.

2. Canister Gas Stoves

Backpacking stoves that sit atop a lightweight cartridge of butane or mixed gas are light, tiny, and burn clean and hot instantly—except in very cold weather, where they are not reliable. Less common are canister-gas "range-top" type stoves more suitable for car camping. The fuel weighs less than liquid fuel for an equal amount of heat produced, but proprietary cartridge designs may not be compatible across stove brands.

3. Propane Stoves

Propane is sold in two kinds of containers: 16.4-ounce steel bottles (about the size of a coffee can) that cannot be refilled, and 20-pound refillable tanks of the type used for barbecue grills. Even the smaller bottles are too heavy for backpacking. Both one- and two-burner propane stoves are popular choices for car and boat camping, however. They are easy to light, require no priming, and the large tanks will last for weeks. Their stability and large surface area allow the use of conventional kitchen cookware, and some have foldable legs and accessory grills.

Other Stoves

Other stove types are available to burn alcohol or small bits of wood, but these are favored mainly by small minorities of backpackers interested in going "ultralight." Although they are valid options, we recommend that beginning campers stick to the more common choices of white gas, canister gas, or propane.

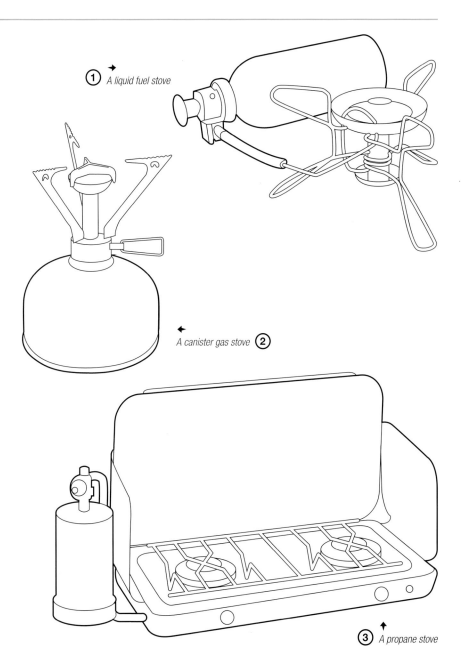

1 *A liquid fuel stove*

A canister gas stove 2

3 *A propane stove*

Planning

Gear

Techniques

Hazards

Hiking

Camping with Kids

Stove Types and Fuels

Fuel	Advantages	Disadvantages	Requires priming and/or pressurizing?	Stove notes
White Gas	• Burns hot • Spills are quick to evaporate • Some white gas stoves can burn other fuels	• Fuel is expensive, volatile, may produce soot • Noisy	• Yes	• Backpacker and camp stoves readily available • Maintenance and spare parts are critical to reliability
Propane	• Mechanically simple • Relatively inexpensive • Easy to light • Large tanks hold fuel for long trips	• Heavier than liquid fuel stoves • Fuel containers are heavy • 16.4-oz bottles not refillable	• No	• Camp stoves only • Two-burner versions widely available
Butane	• Simple to light • Instant heat • Can be tiny and lightweight	• Canister designs not universal • Availability limited, non-refillable, disposal issues • Not effective in cold weather	• No	• Primarily backpacker stoves

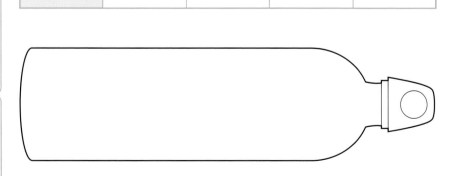

↑
A typical white gas bottle

COOKWARE

As in all other things, backpackers and bike campers strive to minimize volume and weight in their kitchen hardware. An important aspect of this is menu planning, one objective of which is to minimize the amount of cookware required. It's rare that you will bring more than one pot and one fry pan, and common to rely entirely on one or the other. Car and boat campers, having fewer such constraints, can plan more elaborate meals and pack more prodigally.

Cookware for the lightweight crowd is made from thin-gauge steel, aluminum, or even titanium, which is outrageously expensive but extremely durable for its light weight. To conserve space, pots are often just large enough for the number of campers on a trip. To save even more weight and make packing

easier, backpacking cookware often lacks attached handles. Pots are handled with a pliers-like gripper or with a single removable handle that is shared between cookpot and frypan. Car and boat campers, in contrast, often make do with their everyday cookpots, and some go to the opposite extreme, bringing heavy enameled-steel or even cast-iron cookware.

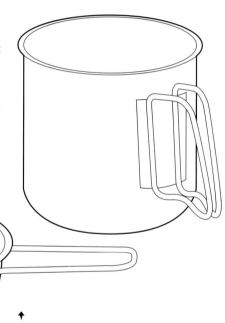

A lightweight, one-person cookpot/fry pan set

Food Preparation

If you're a backwoods gourmet who relishes well-prepared meals and avoids quick-and-dirty expedients, you may not be satisfied with your camping knife for meal preparation. Here is an alternative. Make a temporary sheath from cardboard for a good kitchen knife, and pack a small, thin plastic cutting board of the kind designed for campers.

Planning

Gear

Techniques

Hazards

Hiking

Camping with Kids

Cookware Extras

With few weight constraints, automotive and boat campers often make use of the following cookware, which can turn camp cookery into appealing, distinctive cuisine.

1. Dutch oven: With a bail-like handle and stubby tripod legs, Dutch ovens are designed to be used over campfires or with charcoal. The high rim on the lid contains coals, so that food cooks from above and below. Dutch ovens are capable of producing a huge range of dishes: not just stews and soups, but also casseroles, roasts, and baked goods. Cast-iron ovens cook better; aluminum versions are lighter.

2. Reflector oven: A favorite among boat campers, these foldable sheet-metal contraptions concentrate heat from a campfire to produce baked goods.

3. Pie iron (a.k.a. camp cooker): A hinged pair of heavy metal plates which are attached to long metal poles, into which two slices of bread and fillings are placed.

4. Coffee makers: Drip-style coffee makers are available with a built-in propane burner, or designed to work over a propane stove. Lightweight espresso pots are available for the backpacker who must have his or her refined java drink on the trail.

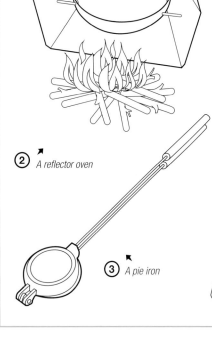

① *A Dutch oven*

② *A reflector oven*

③ *A pie iron*

④ *Camper's espresso maker*

DINNERWARE

Plates and glassware of nonbreakable plastic but normal, everyday size are preferred for car and RV camping, although paper plates and cups will do the job for some menus. Cutlery too can be either the everyday stuff or disposable plastic. Backpackers and bike and boat campers typically prefer lightweight plastic, and will often use a single deep plate or shallow bowl for all meals, regardless of whether it's a solid or liquid dish. Backpackers' cutlery is made from lightweight metals or from high-quality plastic that is meant to be reused indefinitely. Sporks (combination spoons and forks) are popular to save weight and to eliminate one more item from the pack. Since most backpackers carry pocket knives, dinner knives are usually unnecessary.

Washing-Up Gear

Car and boat campers may bring a plastic dishpan for washing up after meals: backpackers and bike campers must use their cooking pots. Bring a pot scrubber in a plastic bag, a small plastic bottle of biodegradable soap, and another bottle with a few ounces of unscented laundry bleach as a disinfectant. Paper towels are handy but bulky. Crush the roll flat before packing, or unroll just enough sheets for your trip and store them in plastic.

Trash Bags

Reuse empty food bags as small trash bags on the trail. Bring one larger, heavy-duty trash bag to contain them all and protect against leakage.

FOOD CONTAINERS

Backpackers, bike campers, and most boat campers avoid canned goods due to their weight, and food in even heavier glass jars or bottles is *forbidden* in most public camping areas due to the danger that broken glass poses to users. Many common packaged foods, however, including tuna and fruit preserves, are available in soft packs or plastic bottles. Non perishable foods like cooking oil and peanut butter that might be purchased in glass can be repackaged in plastic.

Avoid using rigid reusable plastic containers when possible. An old single-serving water bottle makes a good, reliable container for cooking oil that can be crunched flat when it's empty. Peanut butter can be transferred into a zip-lock plastic bag that takes up almost no space. Virtually all dried foods should be removed from boxes and placed in zip-lock bags. Even more space can be saved by repackaging dry foods with a home-style vacuum-sealer.

BEAR BAG

In some areas, food and trash must be protected from bears, raccoons, squirrels, or other pests. In wooded areas, use a bear bag: a strong cloth bag (or a backpack) that you hang by rope from a tree limb out of these scavengers' reach. A small pulley slung over the branch makes it much easier to lift the weight of a pack full of food.

In treeless regions, use a hard plastic bear-proof container. These do a good, but not flawless job of containing food odors that may attract bears, and their rounded shapes with an absence of protrusions make it difficult for bears to tear them open with their claws.

Planning

Gear

Techniques

Hazards

Hiking

Camping with Kids

Water

Those who stay in drive-in campgrounds generally have no special concerns regarding water: it's always there at the tap and it's almost always potable. Backcountry campers are a different story. They must carry or collect sufficient water to rehydrate their dried foods and to replace the water lost through physical activity. Because backcountry water sources are not necessarily safe and potable, they must treat their water before drinking it.

TREATMENT

Even in remote areas, assume that water in lakes and streams is not safe to drink. Aside from man made chemical pollution, you need to be concerned about natural pathogens, especially the protozoans *giardia lamblia* and *cryptosporidium* (known to their friends as giardia and crypto). These can cause giardiasis and cryptosporidiosis, respectively. Both are intestinal illnesses that are spread in mammalian (including human) feces and are extremely unpleasant at the very least—and occasionally deadly.

While any given water source may be safe, if you drink indiscriminately from untreated water, you stand a good chance of eventually becoming ill from these or other pathogens. It is highly recommended, therefore, to treat all water from natural sources before drinking it. There are four main methods:

Boiling: Boiling your water will kill any living pathogen. Outdated advice calls for boiling water for as long as 15 minutes, but more recent research indicates that just bringing the water to a full boil is sufficient. This is good, because it uses much less stove fuel.

Chemicals: Iodine-based chemicals reliably kill waterborne parasites, bacteria, and viruses, but many campers find their taste unpleasant, and it's necessary to wait 15 minutes or longer for the chemical to have its full effect before drinking. Consuming too much iodine is a health risk, so this should be considered a backup measure in case your primary treatment system fails.

Filtering: Filters designed for campers remove giardia and crypto, along with most bacteria and particulates, but not viruses. Most filters operate with a hand pump, but some are gravity-fed. Some filters deposit small measured doses of iodine to kill viruses without causing a health risk from the chemical itself.

Ultraviolet sterilization: UV light will reliably kill pathogens, including viruses. The systems rely on electric power, which may be provided by batteries or by a hand-cranked dynamo.

CARRYING WATER

Few campers rely on the traditional military-style canteen any more. For carrying a small quantity of water—enough for an individual to drink on the trail—wide-mouth plastic water bottles offer advantages: they're easier to fill and clean; you can see how much they contain; you can add powdered drink mix to them; and they avoid the unpleasant taste that metal canteens impart to water. If the small mouth doesn't put you off, then empty single-serving soda bottles work well. They're light, durable, and they cost nothing.

Another option for carrying your own water is the hydration bladder. These rugged plastic bags slip into a special sleeve in many backpacks. Emerging from the bag is a hose that terminates with a "bite valve." Biting

Water Treatment Methods

Treatment	Pros	Cons
Boiling	• Highly reliable • Kills all biological pathogens • Hot water is useful anyway	• Does not remove particulates • Takes time • Consumes fuel • Unpleasant taste • Cooling time if hot water is not desired
Filtering	• Convenient • Removes particulates • Hand-pumping is a continuous, non batch process • Treat as much as you wish	• Hand-pumping requires work • Maintenance required • Pumps subject to malfunction • Does not eliminate viruses
Chemicals	• Compact • Convenient • Kills all pathogens	• Does not remove particulates • Unpleasant taste • Health risk • Waiting time
Ultraviolet Light	• Convenient • Kills all pathogens	• Does not remove particulates • Most systems require batteries

down on the valve opens it, and then you can suck water through the hose. By clipping the hose to your shirt, jacket, or backpack strap, you can take a hands-free sip of water whenever you want without stopping to fumble with a bottle.

Canoe campers often carry collapsible water jugs that hold from 1 to 5 gallons. The benefit of a large container like this is that you can filter all the water you need for a large group just once a day. A lower-cost alternative is a plastic one-gallon milk jug with a screw-on top. These are lightweight and surprisingly durable, but bulky.

Car campers and RVers usually take their water from the campground tap. But if you're *boondocking* (RV camping outside of an established campground) and will need more water than your tanks can hold, carry it in 5-gallon plastic jerricans and make sure they're well-secured: you don't want 45-pound missiles flying around inside your vehicle should you need to stop short.

← Hand-operated water filter

Planning

Gear

Techniques

Hazards

Hiking

Camping with Kids

Health and Hygiene

Many of us spend little time outdoors, and most of us are not as active as we should be. When camping, we expose ourselves to the weather to a greater extent than usual, and subject our bodies to unaccustomed activities. We also face the challenge of maintaining good hygiene in unaccustomed circumstances. Packing the proper gear is the first step toward meeting these challenges and maintaining good health.

FIRST AID

Without medical training and specialized equipment, the only medical treatment possible in the field is first aid. First aid consists of generally simple procedures that, in and of themselves, suffice to treat many minor injuries. If the injury is more serious, first aid stabilizes the situation, preventing the injury from becoming worse and minimizing pain until professional medical treatment can be obtained.

Basic first-aid training, widely available through the American Red Cross, is highly desirable preparation for any camping trip that will take you several hours away from the nearest medical treatment. It is also advisable to bring a first-aid guide into the field for reference in situations with which you are unfamiliar. (See Resources, page 183.)

Assembling a Kit

Pre-assembled first-aid kits are available at any drug store. Think of these as a potentially good starting point for your camping first-aid kit. They may be an economical first step to collecting some of the tools and supplies you need, but they are almost certainly not complete and adequate for your needs.

To develop the complete list of your needs, see the checklist on page 181, and consider the variables of your trip and your party:
- What are the environmental factors and risks (venomous animals, poisonous plants, extreme heat or cold, high altitude, infectious diseases, etc.)?

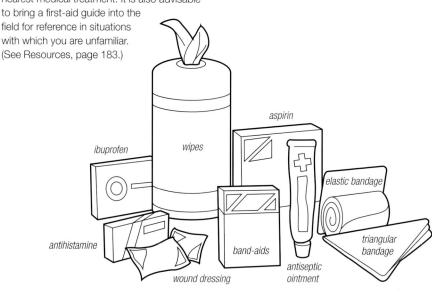

aspirin

ibuprofen

wipes

elastic bandage

antihistamine

band-aids

triangular bandage

wound dressing

antiseptic ointment

- What physical activities may entail special risks (axe use, rock climbing, fishing, bicycling, campfires, etc.)?
- What medical skills does your party possess (has anyone ever sutured a wound, administered an injection, set a fracture, made an incision, etc.)?
- What are the special medical needs of the individuals (diabetes, asthma, allergies, heart condition, history of sprained ankles, ear infections, bad back, varicose veins, etc.)?

Taking these factors into consideration, compile a list of foreseeable injuries, illnesses, and medical conditions that might need treatment, with the appropriate instruments, medicines, and supplies beside each problem.

Packing Your Kit

You may find that the list becomes unreasonably long, so that an entire backpack would have to be devoted to carrying it. Make careful, reasoned judgments about where to cut back: about what problems are most likely; what problems would absolutely require treatment; and what supplies might serve double-duty. (For example, while the painkillers aspirin, acetaminophen, and ibuprofen each have advantages in certain situations, you might be able to get by with just one of them.) If you're starting with a pre-stocked kit, you can remove what you don't need to make room for something else: ditch excess adhesive bandages; squeeze half of the antibiotic ointment out of the tube and discard it.

A plastic box makes a better container than a stuff sack: items tend to remain more orderly, and when you open the lid, you can more readily find what you're looking for. Take special measures to keep your kit dry. If you use a plastic tackle box, pack it inside a large zip-lock plastic bag. Boaters should go a step further, placing the kit inside a dry bag, or using a rigid container with a waterproof seal of the type used for cameras and electronic equipment.

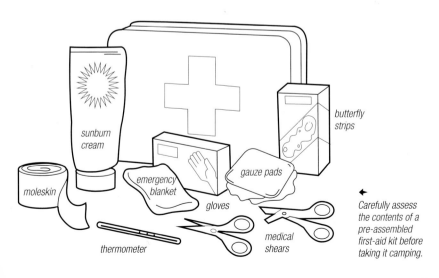

sunburn cream

butterfly strips

moleskin

emergency blanket

gloves

gauze pads

thermometer

medical shears

← *Carefully assess the contents of a pre-assembled first-aid kit before taking it camping.*

Personal First-Aid Kit

In addition to the comprehensive kit for the group, each adult camper should consider carrying a compact kit for minor incidents and personal needs. These might contain just a few adhesive bandages, a gauze pad, a small roll of waterproof tape, a pouch of antibiotic ointment, a few aspirin tablets, and perhaps allergy pills or heart medication. All this can be stored in a plastic container smaller than a sandwich and carried in a shirt pocket or waist pack.

The Toilet

Drive-in campgrounds usually have bathrooms with flush toilets or, failing that, well-accommodated outhouses. Car campers who wish to avoid these public restrooms can bring a chemical toilet. Many backcountry camping areas—especially the more popular ones—have outhouses near every established campsite.

Some of the more remote and less-visited wilderness areas provide no facilities at all. In most such places, it is acceptable to bury your feces. If you'll be moving to a different campsite every night, then a small trowel will suffice to dig a single-use "cat hole." A standard garden trowel will do the job, but a plastic campers' version will save several ounces in your pack. If your group is a large one, however, or if you plan to spend a few days in a single campsite, then you must dig a latrine. A military-style folding entrenching tool is a good size and weight for this purpose.

Burial of waste is prohibited in some wilderness areas, in which case it must either be bagged and packed out, or a camp toilet used to contain it. Toilets are available in two popular versions, the simpler and cheaper of which is a 5-gallon plastic bucket with a removable seat and a snap-tight lid. A slightly more sophisticated style has folding legs that support a seat at the height of a conventional toilet. A plastic bag is suspended beneath the seat, and the whole rig folds into a briefcase-size box. Both types of toilets can benefit from the addition of a special chemical powder or cat litter to absorb odor and liquids.

Few backcountry outhouses are stocked with toilet paper, so bring your own. Crush the roll flat to save space and pack it in a zip-lock bag.

Environmental Protection

Don't forget to pack these items to protect yourself from the environment:

☐ sunglasses
☐ sunblock
☐ zinc oxide cream: An extremely effective form of sunblock for sensitive areas like the upper lip and the tips of your ears
☐ bug repellent (a.k.a. bug dope): In addition to the kind you apply to your skin or clothing, some campers bring citronella candles or slow-burning chemical coils that release a repellent into the air, to keep bugs away from the dining area.
☐ head net or bug suit: In areas where mosquitoes are particularly bad, chemical warfare often doesn't suffice, and the only way to protect yourself is to cover all exposed skin with netting.

Soap

Backcountry campers disagree about soap. Some feel that any soap used when camping pollutes the environment. These conscientious souls typically wash with plain water, scrubbing themselves vigorously with a washcloth. If you choose to use soap, use the biodegradable camping variety, and take care to keep it away from water sources.

Carrying it All

Your mode of transport determines how you will pack your gear. Each type of camping has developed special bags, boxes, and techniques that work well for that particular camping style.

CAR CAMPING AND RVING

Most RVs are well-equipped with closets, drawers, and cabinets designed and outfitted to keep everything safe and in place when under way, and easily accessible in camp. Should more room be needed, weatherproof storage boxes are available to mount over the rear bumper, over the tongue on some travel trailers, or in the bed of a pickup truck tow vehicle.

Most car campers prefer side-zip duffel bags for personal gear because they use trunk space more efficiently than semi-rigid suitcases. Don't get the old military-style canvas duffel that opens only at one end: whatever you need is invariably at the bottom, requiring that everything else be dumped out to get to it. Each camper should have his or her own bag, and this includes even the youngest children. Throw in a few plastic bags to protect wet clothing, muddy shoes, and the like.

Plastic totes of 15–25 gallons work well for most of the communal gear like the kitchen, first-aid kit, tarp, rope, and hatchet.

BOAT CAMPING

Boat campers need luggage that will pack efficiently into the boat and can be portaged easily. Most backpacks are out because they are not waterproof, and because their suspension systems limit their flexibility. The old-fashioned frameless canvas Duluth pack—now available in modern materials as well—will conform to the shape of any available space, and a waterproof liner will provide protection for most flatwater situations. Whitewater boaters must pack virtually everything in dry bags or boxes. Large dry bags are available with shoulder straps for easy portaging. Dry boxes require an accessory harness with shoulder straps.

Favored almost exclusively by traditional canoeists, wannigans are non waterproof boxes designed to fit precisely into the boat's midship section. Though heavy and difficult to portage, they make efficient use of space, and can double as a seat or food-prep counter in camp. Most sea kayakers pack their gear in dry bags, because deck hatches are often not completely waterproof.

The table on the following page shows the choices favored by most experienced boat campers.

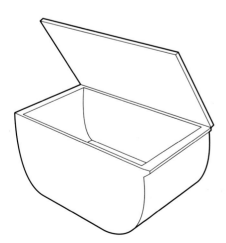

← *A wannigan*

Planning

Gear

Techniques

Hazards

Hiking

Camping with Kids

↟
A Duluth pack

↟
Dry bags

Packing options for boat camping

Gear type	Dry bag	Dry box	Pack basket	Duluth pack	Wannigan	Other non-waterproof bag
Clothing	R, WC, WK, SK, F		F	F		SK
Kitchen	R, WC, WK, SK, F	R		F	F	SK
Tents	R, WC, WK	R		F		R, WC, WK, SK, F
Sleeping bags/pads	R, WC, WK, SK, F	R		F		SK
Food	WC, WK, SK	R	F	F	F	SK
Misc. water-tolerant			F	F		R, WC, WK, SK, F

R = whitewater raft / WC = whitewater canoe / WK = whitewater kayak / SK = sea kayak / F = flatwater canoe

↑
Bike with front and rear panniers

BIKE CAMPING

Bike campers can pack their gear in panniers, on a trailer or, rarely, both. Among a long list of pros and cons for both options: panniers are less expensive and lighter, but when loaded, they alter the balance of the bicycle; trailers also affect handling and braking, but in different ways from panniers; four panniers can hold more gear than a trailer, but they create more drag.

Pairs of panniers are clipped to lightweight metal racks that mount above the rear, and sometimes the front, wheel. Most panniers have a good degree of water resistance, but in rainy country, it's wise to pack your sleeping bag in a waterproof stuff sack as well. Additional gear can be strapped to the rack itself. A smaller bag that straps to the handlebar is usually reserved for items requiring quick access on the road.

Trailers are pulled from a trailer hitch that is bolted to the bike frame, and gear is carried on the trailer in a weatherproof bag.

Planning

Gear

Techniques

Hazards

Hiking

Camping with Kids

BACKPACKING

External-frame packs have a rigid metal (or on the odd occasion, plastic) frame to which the bag itself is fastened on one side, and a system of straps on the other. Internal-frame packs have springy metal stays buried in the structure of the bag, between the straps and the cargo compartment.

The frame functions to distribute weight from your shoulders to other parts of your body, and is essential for carrying heavy loads long distances. (Packs without frames are okay for day hiking and short hauls.) Most backpackers quickly develop a strong preference for either external- or internal-frame packs, although they each have advantages in different situations.

Internal-frame packs (sometimes shortened to "internal packs") are narrower and hug the body more closely, making them better suited to conditions that require careful maneuvring and balance. External-frame packs (or simply, "frame packs") provide better air circulation to your back and so are more comfortable in hot weather. Most internal packs are top-loading, so you have to dig for your gear. External-frame packs have a greater number of discrete compartments, both front- and top-loading. This provides easier

access to gear and tends to keep it better organized. Frame packs are also more comfortable with very heavy loads, and tend to be less expensive.

Strange to say, internal-frame packs are much more popular. Perhaps this is because they are the newer, sexier design and are associated with the high adventure of mountaineering. While internal-frame packs certainly have some advantages, don't overlook the virtues of the less fashionable, less expensive, highly capable external-frame pack.

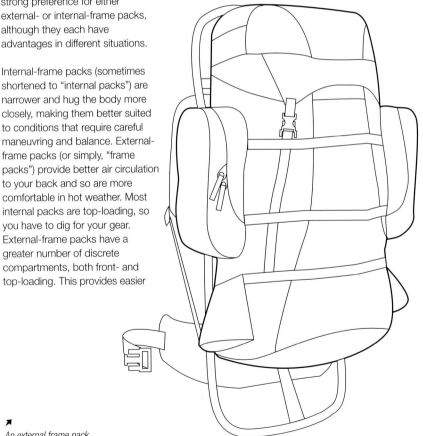

↗
An external frame pack

Pack Size

While a pack must be big enough to carry your gear, you don't want one bigger or heavier than necessary. Weekend campers need a pack of 1,830–3,050 cubic inches capacity. For trips up to five nights or so, a 4,575 cubic inches pack will be plenty. Don't go above that unless you need to carry a lot of specialized gear or plan to be out for weeks.

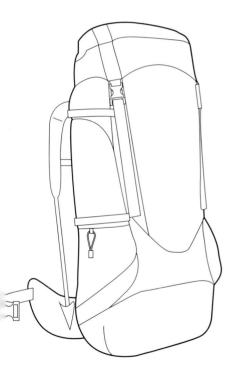

↗
An internal frame pack

Backpack Features

When choosing a backpack, consider the value of these features while bearing in mind that most of them add weight:

☐ **Integral rain cover:** If one isn't included, consider buying one as a separate accessory.

☐ **Lots of pockets and compartments:** Helps to keep things organized and provides convenient access, but you have to remember which pocket the desired item is in.

☐ **"Hydration compatibility":** A special sleeve or hook holds your water bladder upright, and a grommeted hole through the pack wall allows you to route the sipping tube so that it's in easy reach as you walk.

☐ **Hip belt:** A well-padded hip belt is essential for serious backpacking. It allows you to carry much of the weight on your hips, taking weight off your back and shoulders.

☐ **Ergonomic shoulder straps:** Curve nicely around your shoulder joints for greater comfort and ease of movement.

☐ **Chest strap/Sternum strap:** Keeps the shoulder straps from spreading, and transfers some weight to your chest.

☐ **Tump line:** Fastens around your forehead, allowing your neck muscles to bear part of the weight.

Essentials to Pack

All types of campers—automotive, boat, bike, and backpack—should have a daypack or a large waist pack in which to carry a spare jacket, a snack, a water bottle, a first-aid kit, and a survival kit during short excursions away from the campsite.

Signaling

If you're lost or injured, making yourself seen or heard is often the best way out of trouble. While many of us enjoy camping for its escape from the modern world, most signaling methods involve the use of electronics.

VOICE COMMUNICATIONS

Many popular camping areas have good cellphone coverage in heavily used areas, but it typically drops off to "zero bars" once you get into the backcountry. Satellite phones are good everywhere on Earth (except perhaps near the poles), but are too expensive for most campers.

Handheld two-way radios that operate in the UHF band are handy to maintain communication within your party, as long as you remain within range of one another. Distance is usually not a problem, as many small, inexpensive units now boast ranges of 15 miles or more, but this assumes an unobstructed line of sight between units. In most situations, trees, hills, and other obstructions cut the effective range of units down considerably.

The bigger problem, however, is that the parties in a group can generally talk only to each other. You can't call the park ranger, police, coast guard, or anyone else with a two-way UHF radio, because they're not listening to your channel. They can be very useful, however, for children to stay in touch with parents when they go exploring away from the campsite.

Marine-style VHF radios are practical for sea kayakers because they transmit over channels monitored by the U.S. Coast Guard. With that exception, there are few good voice communications technologies for campers to call for outside help.

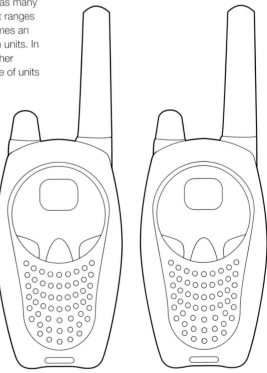

Two-way radios

Planning

Gear

Techniques

Hazards

Hiking

Camping with Kids

LOCATOR BEACONS

Personal locator beacons use GPS technology and satellite communications to send a distress call to either an emergency-rescue service, or a pre-set phone number or email address. About the size of a small handheld radio, they do not support voice communications (at this time) and are used only to communicate location. They can be programmed to transmit your location at a certain time every day, so that friends at home can track your progress. Or, at the touch of a button, you can send a distress signal. It won't indicate the nature of your problem, only that you need help. They are somewhat costly (especially the required monthly subscription fees), and are generally considered practical only for lengthy expeditions into remote areas.

OLD-SCHOOL SIGNALING TECHNOLOGY

Many backcountry campers carry two old standby signaling devices: a small steel mirror and a whistle. On a clear, sunny day, the mirror can be used to reflect sunlight toward a search party on a distant ridge or in an aircraft. The whistle can make you heard over a longer distance than your voice can carry, at a much smaller expenditure of breath.

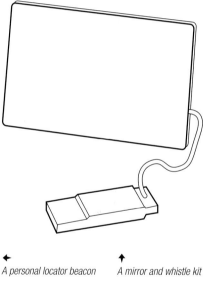

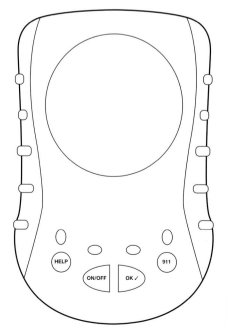

← *A personal locator beacon*   ↑ *A mirror and whistle kit*

VHF Weather-Band Radio

Although only a receiving device, a VHF weather-band radio is a useful tool to pack. They pick up reports transmitted nonstop by the U.S. Weather Service for all areas of the country, and some will set off an alarm in case of a severe-weather warning.

Planning

Gear

Techniques

Hazards

Hiking

Camping with Kids

Navigation

Knowing where you are is only half of navigation: knowing where you're going and how you'll get there is the rest. Even with GPS widely available, map and compass remain important tools for backcountry travel.

MAPS

Car campers and RVers generally need nothing more than a road map to find their way, and GPS, whether as a standalone unit or a smartphone app, has made the process of navigating to the campground easier than ever. Combined with a smartphone's ability to identify every conceivable travel service and tourist attraction along the way, automotive campers should never find themselves lost or at a loss for anything.

Topographic Maps

Bicycle campers are additionally concerned with the slope of the terrain—something not shown on road maps. Topographic maps (and their smartphone app equivalents) show you how much climbing a road requires, so that you can adjust your estimated daily mileage or change your route to a road with a gentler slope.

Backpackers have even greater need for topos, as they provide essential information for finding your location and planning your route. Large-scale maps of 1:24,000 (i.e., one inch on the map represents 24,000 inches on the ground, or 2,000 feet) cover a small area in great detail. These are desirable for steep, complex terrain and for areas where marked trails don't exist. In addition to a highly "granular" view of the topography, they also show the details like water sources and small man made structures. Maps of 1:50,000 to 1:62,500 are often sufficient for areas where hiking trails are better maintained and marked, but still show enough detail to help you out if you lose the trail. Depend upon smaller scales (1:100,000 to 1:130,000)

only if you're sure the trails are well-marked and maintained. They're also useful to know what's beyond the area where you'll camp. Anything over 1:200,000 may be okay for big-picture planning purposes, but don't depend upon it to navigate in the field.

Trail Maps and Guides

The U.S. Geological Survey—the primary source of topographic information in the U.S.—does not maintain a very rigorous schedule for updating its maps, and many contain data that is decades old. More recent information is often available in trail maps and guides of most popular camping areas published by National Geographic, Mountaineers, the Appalachian Mountain Club, and commercial publishers like Falcon Guides and Globe Pequot. Whereas USGS topos are general-purpose maps intended for all types of land users, trail maps and guides are designed especially for backcountry travelers, so they include trail descriptions, campsites and picnic areas, side trails, historical notes, and emergency contact information: they show you what to expect at virtually every turn in the trail.

→

A topographic map (see pages 153–154,

COMPASSES

A compass helps to orient yourself on a map, enabling you to relate the information on the map to the terrain you observe (and vice versa). Two types are common in the backcountry:

Lensatic compasses: Capable of greater precision in sighting a distant land feature.

Baseplate or orienteering compasses: The lighter, less expensive, and more popular of the two among hikers. Their clear plastic base is more easily oriented on a topo map. Compensation for declination (the difference between true and magnetic North) can be performed right on the compass, simplifying an easy but essential mathematical operation.

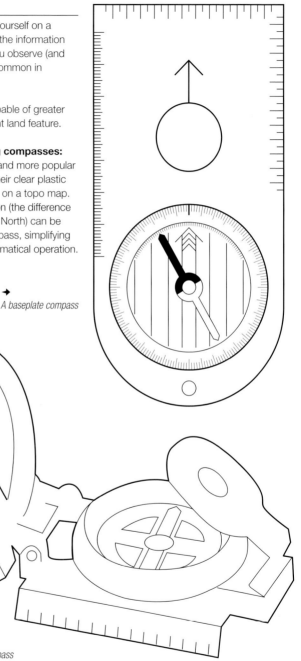

A baseplate compass

A lensatic compass

GPS

GPS is actually the Geostationary Positioning *System*, which consists of a bunch of billion-dollar satellites circling the Earth. The device you buy is a GPS *receiver*, which gathers information transmitted by three or more satellites at a time to calculate your position on the globe. A true GPS receiver works anywhere that it can receive satellite signals. In contrast, the GPS app on your smartphone might not work if you're out of network.

Some GPS receivers can upload programs that provide the details of commercial trail guides and maps and allow you to add notations and waypoints at any location. Compared to map and compass, GPS is easier to use (for most), more comprehensive and more capable, as well as lighter and more compact. Some hikers now depend upon GPS exclusively, but others, who are unwilling to place all their trust in a fallible electronic device, bring map and compass as a backup.

↗
A handheld GPS unit

Planning

Gear

Techniques

Hazards

Hiking

Camping with Kids

More Tools and Supplies

So many tools and supplies are *potentially* useful when camping that the problem is knowing when to stop. Being prepared is only partly about having the right stuff at hand. Knowing how to use it is also important. So is knowing how to make do without it.

CUTTING TOOLS

Almost every camper should carry a knife, as there's always something in need of cutting, whether it's tinder for a campfire or a recalcitrant bag of marshmallows. An axe or a saw may also be worthwhile, but only if you plan to cut wood for fires.

Axes do a better job splitting short lengths of wood and processing kindling. Saws cut through logs much more easily, and they're safer. Unless you can afford the weight of both, you'll have to take your pick.

Knives

Knives that are appropriate for camping may have either folding or fixed blades. Fixed-blade knives, also known as sheath knives, tend to be sturdier, but they are too big to fit in a pocket and must be worn on your belt.

Folding knives can be small enough to fit in your pocket and still big enough to do almost anything you ask of them. Many folding knives, like the popular Swiss Army Knife, have additional tools such as can openers, screwdrivers, awls, and corkscrews, all of which might be useful.

Folding knives that are too large for your pocket are called *belt folders*, and have either a belt clip or a sheath. A *lockback* is a variety of folding knife that has a mechanism to lock the blade in place when it's open. This worthwhile safety feature, found on many belt folders, helps prevent the blade from folding onto the backs of your fingers should you apply pressure in the wrong direction when using the point of the knife to puncture a surface (as when boring a hole).

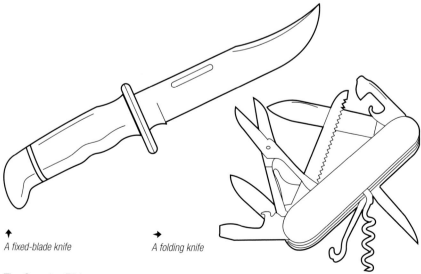

↑
A fixed-blade knife

➜
A folding knife

Another option is the multi-tool, which includes one or more knife blades along with several other tools, usually including robust wire-cutting pliers plus a variety of screwdrivers, wrenches, and more. They differ from Swiss Army-style knives mainly in their emphasis: most multi-tools are pliers first, while their knife blades share second place with many other implements. Swiss Army-type knives are pocket knives that happen to have other functions. Most multi-tools are heavy and bulky compared to pocket knives but not an unreasonable load if carried in a belt sheath.

Knives have such wide general utility—and they are so valuable in a survival situation—that carrying at least two is advisable: one on your person, and one in your pack. A small sharpening stone or one of the new sharpening "files" embedded with abrasive diamond dust should come along on any trip lasting more than a few days.

Axes

Most hatchets, or one-handed axes, have handles about 12 inches long and heads that weigh about 1 pound—which is all that most backpackers are willing to carry. Camp axes, with handles up to 24 inches long and heads weighing up to 2 pounds, are a reasonable load for boat and car campers. The larger axe can be managed with two hands, making it both safer and more powerful, and far more effective at splitting firewood. Larger axes with heads weighing 4 pounds or more and handles greater than 28 inches are impractical for campers.

Every axe must have a sheath. If the axe will see much use over a period of several days, a pocket-size sharpening stone is good to have.

Binding Materials

Bring 25 to 50 feet of strong rope, which is useful in endless ways, such as rigging a tarp, hanging a bear bag, drying clothes, and carrying bundles of firewood. Ten feet or so of string, parachute cord, and/or baling wire is good to have for small gear repairs, spare boot laces, suspending a flashlight in the tent, etc. A full roll of duct tape may be overkill, but by all means bring some of this indispensable material. Unroll a few yards and wrap it around a flashlight, tent pole, or other cylindrical item.

Saws

Boat and car campers have always been able to rely on a variety of bow saws, most of which break down to reasonably compact dimensions for travel. Only recently have saws become practical for backpackers, with the introduction of new, even more compact, collapsible designs.

Camp saws with blades that fold into the handle, like a big pocket knife, are not big enough to process firewood efficiently, but they work well to cut small branches from dead, fallen trees.

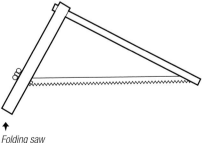

↑
Folding saw

Planning

Gear

Techniques

Hazards

Hiking

Camping with Kids

Optics

Every camper should have his or her own flashlight and every camping party should carry a few spares. Test batteries at home and bring spares. LED flashlights are brighter, use less power, and are less likely to fail than traditional incandescent lamps. Most campers find headlamps more convenient than handheld flashlights for the purposes of cooking, reading, and other activities that require two hands.

Lanterns are nice to have for communal activities like eating together or card games. Lanterns that burn white gas or propane put out a lot of light but are too large for hikers and bikers. (They're also noisy.) Until recently, self-powered campers had no good options, but battery-powered LED lanterns are now available in compact packages.

If you're lost without your glasses, bring a spare pair. The same goes for contact lens wearers, along with the necessary cleaning supplies. In addition:
- All campers should bring sunglasses.
- A bottle of eye-drops belongs in your first-aid kit.
- Binoculars are important for safety and navigation, or consider a monocular to save weight.
- Many campers bring a camera for personal satisfaction.

Repair Kit

Backcountry campers should have a small pouch or box designated for repair items. Contents will vary with the nature of the trip, but may include:

☐ sewing kit
☐ spare zipper pulls for tent, backpack
☐ air mattress patch kit
☐ canoe or raft patch kit
☐ string, cord, baling wire
☐ duct tape
☐ wire-cutter pliers
☐ boot adhesive
☐ tent seam sealant
☐ stove repair kit
☐ tent pole repair sleeve

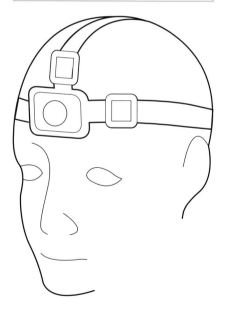

Headlamps free both hands and are always aimed in the direction you're looking.

Emergency/Survival Kit

Since all of your camping gear is intended to help you survive "out there," what's the sense of a separate survival kit? It's insurance: something to carry on your person at all times, just in case you should be separated from the bulk of your gear. Stuff happens: canoes can be lost in rapids; bears get into food bags. Car campers who remain within the campground may think they need never worry about such eventualities, but if a day-hike away from civilization is on the agenda, then even they should be prepared for the unexpected.

THE CONTAINER

Your survival kit must be extremely compact if you're going to carry it at all times. A small, dedicated waist pack works well if you'll be carrying no other packs. To get it any smaller than that—small enough, say, to fit into the cargo pocket of your favorite hiking pants—requires even more careful consideration of what you'll need and what you can do without.

Choosing the box, bag, or other container for the kit can proceed "tops-down" or "bottoms-up." Either select the container you want to carry and then figure out how much you can fit into it, or collect your gear and then choose the smallest container that will hold it all.

Survival Knives

Some so-called "survival knives" feature a hollow handle with a few survival tools stored inside. These knives are often of low quality, bigger than you need, and the "kits" are severely constrained by the space available in the knife's handle. You'll do better by buying a smaller, high-quality knife and assembling your own kit.

There are dozens of pre-stocked emergency survival kits available commercially, but every one of these is based on the manufacturer's guess about what you might find useful or essential. Read the contents of these kits for ideas, then decide for yourself. If a kit suits your needs *mostly*, buy it and then modify its contents to suit.

↗
A survival kit small enough to fit in a shirt pocket can be assembled in an Altoids tin.

Planning

Gear

Techniques

Hazards

Hiking

Camping with Kids

The Contents

A survival kit containing every item on the following list would be too large, but they're all worth considering. Some items were already listed in the previous chapter under "Repair Kit," and this duplication is intentional. You don't want to strip essential gear from your survival kit in the course of making everyday repairs. Any time you use an item from the survival kit, make sure you replace it before your next camping trip.

Fire: Waterproof matches, disposable lighter, flint-and-steel kit or high-temperature sparking tool, tinder or fire-starter paste, solid chemical fuel tablets, candle stub.

Binding: Parachute cord, duct tape, baling wire, sewing thread and needle (dental floss is a good strong substitute for thread).

Cutting: Pocket knife or multi-tool, wire saw, razor blade, X-Acto blade.

First aid: Bandages, antiseptic, antibiotic ointment, pain killer.

Signaling: Steel mirror, whistle.

Compass: A small backup unit will do.

Shelter: Mylar emergency blanket, large plastic trash bag, polyethylene tube tent.

Light: Miniature flashlight, chemical light stick.

Fishing, trapping: 10 yards of monofilament line, split shot, swivel, small hooks, flexible wire for snares.

Food: Energy bars or gels, salt tablets, iodine tablets for water purification, plastic bag to carry water, steel cup for cooking and drinking, aluminum foil for cooking.

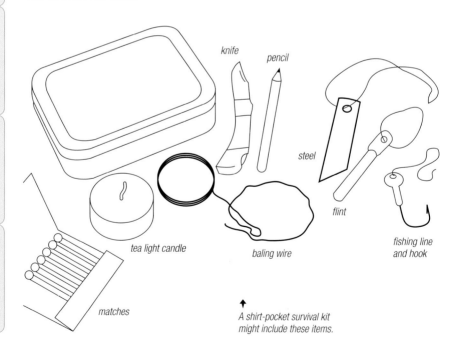

knife

pencil

steel

flint

fishing line and hook

tea light candle

baling wire

matches

↑
A shirt-pocket survival kit might include these items.

Packing for Fun

After packing all the essentials, you still might have a few cubic inches left for discretionary items. After all, camping is supposed to be fun. Everyone enjoys the outdoors for their own reasons, so what follows is simply a list of suggestions of the kinds of extracurricular activities you might enjoy and what you might bring along to pursue them.

Extracurricular Activities

Literary: Books, e-reader, journal.

Games: Cards, board games, puzzles.

Sports: Frisbee, soccer, baseball/softball, badminton, Nerf balls, swimsuit, swim toys.

Fishing: No end to the list of tackle you might bring.

Birdwatching: Binoculars, spotting scope, field guide, journal.

More optical pursuits: Photography, astronomy (compact telescope, planisphere, laser pointer).

More nature: Field guides (flowers, trees, geology, insects, etc.), collecting kits, journal. (Note: collecting specimens is prohibited in many public areas).

Music: Harmonica, backpacker's guitar, violin, flute, recorder, etc., songbook for sing-alongs, MP3 player with ear buds.

Art: Watercolors, sketchbook, whittling knives

Don't forget: Your child's second-favorite toy. (Leave #1 at home for safe-keeping.)

These other nonessentials are too big for backpackers and mostly for consideration by car campers and RVers.

Bicycle: A near-necessity for children of a certain age in drive-in campgrounds. Some well-equipped campgrounds have skateboard ramps. Remember helmet, elbow and knee pads.

Folding camp chairs: Much more comfortable than rocks or logs for sitting around the campfire.

Screen house: If you want to enjoy the outdoors without the bugs.

Kitchen stand/caddy: Folding prep table with space for utensils.

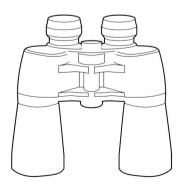

➜ *Binoculars are a valuable navigation tool and also useful for birdwatching and astronomy.*

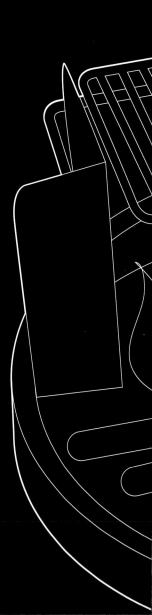

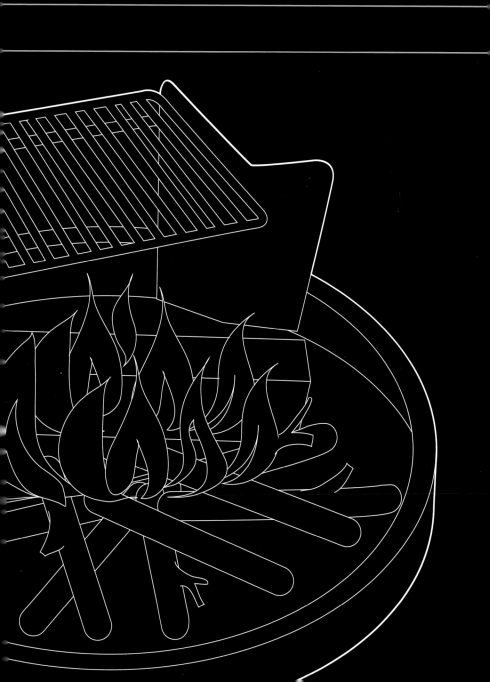

Organizing and Packing

Organizing your gear is an exercise in balancing numerous, sometimes conflicting, priorities. Everything should be easy to find and quick to access—which means you'd like everything to be on top, but that's clearly impossible. Many items need to be kept dry or protected from breakage, which inevitably restricts access. Even the items that clamor for first priority—raingear, first-aid kit, trail snacks, water, map and compass, camera—may be too numerous to allow instant access to all.

BACKPACK PACKING

Try to keep your load to about one-fourth of your body weight, and certainly not above one-third. Overweight folks and young children should stay toward the bottom of that range, while particularly fit individuals can go toward the high end. In calculating your load, include the weight of the pack itself. In practice, this means that most adults will carry from 30 to 50 pounds.

Each individual typically carries his or her own personal gear (clothing, toilet articles, sleeping bag and pad, water) plus some part of the communal gear (kitchen, food, fuel, tent, first-aid and repair kits). Consider distributing the food load and any backup gear, such as a second stove, so that the loss of one backpack doesn't jeopardize the group's safety. It's not terribly important that the group's main cook carry the kitchen, but if one of the party is highly skilled in first aid, it makes good sense for that individual to carry the medical kit.

In external-frame packs, heavy items (including food) should be packed as high as possible and close to the hiker's back. This transfers weight most effectively to the hip belt. Because internal-frame packs are designed to hug the body more closely for better balance, heavy items should be concentrated midway between top and bottom—again as close to the hiker's back as possible, while taking care that hard or sharp items, like stoves and pot handles, are not in

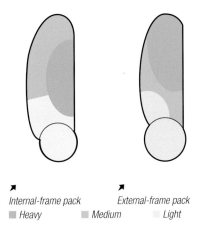

Internal-frame pack   *External-frame pack*
■ *Heavy*   ■ *Medium*   ▫ *Light*

contact with the hiker's back. In situations where balance is of particular concern, move heavy items lower in both types of packs.

Sleeping bags go in the bottom of the pack, while tents are typically strapped outside, below the lowest compartment. If the poles stick out too far horizontally, separate them from the tent body and strap them vertically to the side of the pack. Sleeping pads are also often strapped vertically outside the pack, and you might roll the pad around the poles for protection. Except for the tent poles, all of these items should be protected in waterproof stuff sacks. Plastic zip-lock bags or stuff sacks are also a good idea for clothing and food inside the pack, both for added water protection and as an aid to organization.

Planning

Gear

Techniques

Hazards

Hiking

Camping with Kids

Place bottles of liquid fuel in external pockets so that any leakage will not get into food or clothing. If the pack does not have a hydration sleeve, place your water bottle in another external pocket, opposite the fuel bottle for good balance. Place items that will be needed along the trail in other external pockets: snacks, map, sunblock, bug dope, first-aid kit. Your compass should always be instantly available, so tie a string to it and hang it around your neck.

In the top of the pack, either just beneath the top flap or in an outside pocket, place outerwear that might be needed along the trail (raingear, a fleece jacket) and your pack's rain cover. If you don't strap the tent outside the pack, place it near the top so that, in the case of an unexpected storm, you can set it up without having to unpack and expose other gear to the rain.

BOAT PACKING

Boat campers also carry their personal gear in individual bags, but can devote whole bags or containers to communal gear: typically one for the kitchen, one for food, and one for tents and tools.

To maintain optimum manoeuvrability, sea kayakers should pack light gear (clothing) toward the ends, and heavy gear (food, water), as close to midships as possible. Canoeists should follow roughly the same guidelines, although the ends of a canoe do not offer much space for gear stowage.

Access to the ends of sea kayaks is difficult, so place nothing there that might be needed in a hurry. If you can't reach into the ends through the hatches, tie ropes to your dry bags before pushing them into the ends with a stick. Leave the ropes trailing toward the hatch opening so that you can pull the gear out.

Avoid lashing camping gear on the deck of a kayak. It will reduce the boat's stability and contribute to "windage," allowing the wind to push the boat around more. Similarly, canoeists should keep the top of the load below the gunwales. If there is any prospect of a capsize, gear must be lashed *down*, so that it remains inside the hull. Simply tying or clipping the gear to a thwart or gunwale will not accomplish this, and will make righting the hull significantly more difficult.

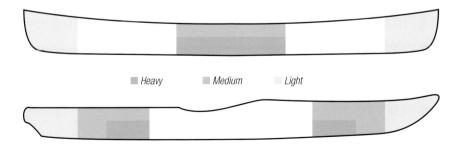

■ *Heavy*　■ *Medium*　■ *Light*

↑
How to load a canoe (top) and a kayak (bottom)

Planning

Gear

Techniques

Hazards

Hiking

Camping with Kids

BIKE PACKING

Most bike trailers have a cargo limit of 70 to 100 pounds. One hundred pounds is a lot to pull, and you should try to pack lighter. Dry bags for bike trailers tend to have few pockets or dividers, so most items go into the same compartment. Keep things organized with stuff sacks. Place heavy items as low as possible and, in the case of two-wheeled trailers, directly above the axle.

When packing panniers, heavy items should go as low and as close to the bike as possible. Weight should be evenly distributed left-to-right, and rear bags should be heavier than front bags. Again, stuff sacks are useful to maintain organization. Because cycling shoes should only be used for cycling, pack a pair of sneakers or sandals near the top of a pannier for easy accessibility.

Many bike-campers place their sleeping bag and pad in waterproof stuff sacks and lash them to the rear rack with bungee cords. This is a good place for these items, since their light weight won't significantly raise the bike's center of gravity. Others prefer to pack them into panniers, primarily as a method of weight control, reasoning that if you place these bulky items inside the bags, there's that much less room for other gear that you can make yourself do without.

Use the handlebar pack for items you'll need during the day or while riding: map, GPS, raingear, snack, wallet, sunblock, cellphone, pocket knife, headlamp.

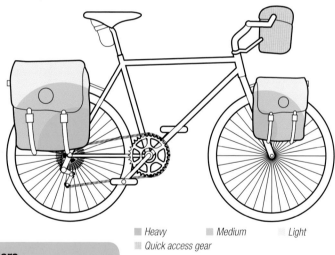

↗
How to load a bike

■ *Heavy*   ■ *Medium*   ▦ *Light*
▦ *Quick access gear*

Cartop Carriers

When car-camping, try to resist the temptation to bring more than you'll use or might realistically need. A weatherproof box or bag mounted on roof racks allows you to pack almost endless gear and toys, and you can fill unused seats with yet more gear. It's not a good idea to have so much that you can't find what you're looking for. If you do use a cartop carrier, bring a footstool for ease of loading.

Making Camp

Choose and set up your campsite properly, and you'll likely have a pleasant stay and remain comfortable regardless of the weather. Do it poorly, and . . . well . . . the opposite.

SELECTING A CAMPSITE

Site selection is rarely an issue for on-the-road campers. Pull up to the campground office and they'll assign you a spot appropriate to your vehicle and the size of your party. This applies to some regulated backwoods camping areas too, where hikers and boat campers are assigned specific campsites for each night out.

Even where sites are not assigned, many backwoods areas allow camping only in established campsites, so much of the thinking has been done for you. You can plan your day's travel to end up at a particular site. Detailed trail guides may describe the pros and cons of individual sites (e.g., view, quality of the ground, distance to the toilet), but if you don't have that information, you'll probably travel until you're tired and take what's there.

Site selection becomes a matter of discretion, then, mainly if you're camping outside of established campsites. Still, if you have a choice between established sites, you might consider these variables:

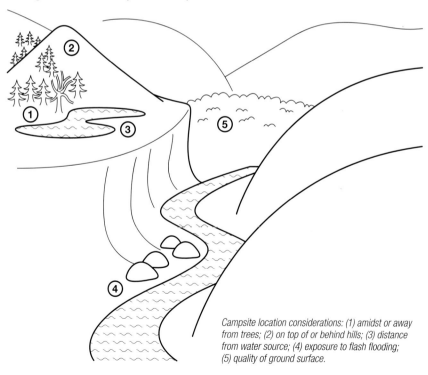

Campsite location considerations: (1) amidst or away from trees; (2) on top of or behind hills; (3) distance from water source; (4) exposure to flash flooding; (5) quality of ground surface.

Planning

Gear

Techniques

Hazards

Hiking

Camping with Kids

Tree Coverage

Trees are a multidimensional issue. It's shadier and generally more pleasant to camp amidst a stand of trees. However, after rain, trees may continue to drip for hours. Trees help break the wind, which is desirable in cool or stormy weather, and unwelcome in hot weather and in areas where mosquitoes gather. Trees can be handy as tying-off points for tarps and clotheslines, although some camping areas prohibit this practice. (Never drive a nail into a tree to hang something from!) Before setting up under a tree, examine it carefully for dead, dangling branches that could fall, using binoculars if necessary.

Wind Exposure

As mentioned above, wind can be a benefit or a liability. Hilltops, ridges, and lakeshores are generally windy. Protection may be found in valleys, at the base of a hill, or behind a large boulder or rock outcrop. However, wind can behave in unexpected ways. The base of a hill might be as windy as the top, and a shift in wind direction can change the situation entirely.

Proximity to Water

Everyone likes to camp near water for the view, for the sound of a running stream, and for ease of access to a drink, a swim, or fishing. But minimum-impact camping protocols call for camping away from water to minimize your visual impact, to spread impacts to other areas, and to minimize the possibility of pollution. Many experts say you should not wash dishes or use soap within 100 feet (or more) of a water source, but if an established campsite is right on a lakeshore or streamside, the land managers obviously don't expect you to follow that guidance.

Avoid low wet places during mosquito season, because mosquitoes and many other biting insects breed in standing water. Don't camp directly on animal trails leading to water sources, to avoid disturbing their natural behavior. A final water-related concern is vulnerability to flash-flooding. This is generally less of an issue in heavily wooded areas. In dry canyonlands, a rainstorm many miles away can cause a flood that could wash you and your campsite away in seconds without warning.

Ground Surface

The ideal ground on which to set up camp is soft enough to take a tent stake and firm enough to hold it securely. Look for an area that has few or no ground-covering plants that could be damaged by your activities. Leaf-covered areas of forest floor are ideal. Bare earth will become muddy in rain. Soft sand is comfortable to sleep on but requires special measures to pitch a tent. Sand also tends to migrate into tents, sleeping bags, and food, and it can be exhausting to walk on. Bare rock is obviously not a desirable place to make your bed.

SETTING UP CAMP

Camp life revolves around four main activities, each having its own area: sleeping, food preparation, eating, and sanitation.

Division of Labor

Divide chores so that everyone contributes to the effort. Nothing creates resentment and conflict faster than having a few people do all the work while others relax. Depending upon the skills and inclinations of the individuals, you can rotate tasks or assign them permanently. If one person hates to cook (or does it poorly), that individual might take permanent responsibility for setting up the tent or cutting firewood. Or everyone can take turns at all chores. Any child older than a toddler should help in some way, if only by laying out his or her own sleeping bag or gathering kindling.

The Sleeping Area

In addition to the consideration of ground surface, it's pleasant to locate the tent with a nice view out the front flap, and/or visibility of the cooking and eating areas. If bad weather is anticipated, face the entry away from the prevailing wind. In hot, still weather, you might do the opposite, so that any breeze flows freely through the tent.

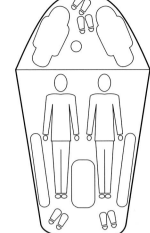

➜

Store boots, backpacks, and water bottles in the vestibule of the tent, keeping your warm clothes in the center of the main compartment with rainwear to the sides. In very cold weather move boots to the main compartment too.

Setting Up a Tent

This book doesn't give directions for setting up tents, because every one is different and all tent manufacturers provide adequate instructions. Here is some advice though:

Staying dry: Minimal-impact ethics advise against the old-school procedure of digging a trench around the tent to divert running water. (It's rarely effective anyway.) Instead, avoid low areas that will become water pathways or collection basins in case of rain.

Ground cloth placement: Some campers place the ground cloth beneath the tent; others place it inside, between the tent floor and the sleeping pads. On sharp pebbles, the ground-cloth-below method may help prevent tears to the tent floor. The ground-cloth-inside method seems to do a better job preventing general long-term wear. If you do place it outside, tuck in the edges so they will not catch rain and channel it beneath the tent.

Pitching in sand: In ground that's too loose to hold a tent stake, use a *deadman*. Tie cords to the tent's corner loops, tie sticks, rocks, or other solid objects with a lot of surface area to the opposite ends, and bury them several inches deep. Do the same with the tent's guylines.

Pitching on rock: On ground that's too hard to take a stake, tie the corner cords and guylines around large (but manageable) rocks, and place another large rock over each cord, directly in front of the first set of rocks to keep them from sliding. The corner cords should be just long enough to accommodate the second rock between the anchor rock and the tent body.

Make your bed: Do this as soon as the tent is up. Inflate your air mattress or, if you have a self-inflating pad, unroll it inside the tent, open the air valve, and let it "breathe" for several minutes before closing the valve. Pull the sleeping bag from its stuff sack and fluff it up to give the insulation as much time as possible to regain its loft before you climb into it for the night.

Planning

Gear

Techniques

Hazards

Hiking

Camping with Kids

D.I.Y. Sink

If you carry water in a large container with a pouring valve, tie it to a tree near the eating or cooking area, 3 or 4 feet off the ground with the valve facing down. It's almost as convenient as a sink with running water. You can leave it there overnight: animals won't bother it.

Food Preparation and Eating Areas

In established backwoods campsites, fire rings and picnic tables are generally adjacent to one another and too close to tent sites. Use the established facilities nonetheless. When setting up your own site, locate the food preparation and eating areas at least 100 feet from the tent to avoid unpleasant interactions with wildlife. The cooking area should be downwind of the tent to keep it safe from smoke, cooking odors, and embers. Movement between the food prep

Pitching a Fly

Food preparation and eating are much more convenient and comfortable in bad weather under a dining fly. Here are some suggestions for pitching it right:

- Support the tarp over a ridge line—a rope tied tightly between two trees—then tie the edges of the tarp out at the grommets. This is much more effective than trying to make the tarp taut by supporting it directly by the grommets.

- Angle the fly so that it will shed water in a convenient direction—for example, away from the path between the cooking area and the eating area.
- If the fly is mostly in a single plane (like a lean-to roof), place a ridge near the upper edge and angle the leading edge downward with guylines. This will minimize flapping.
- Pitching the fly on the bias (with the ridge diagonally between opposite corners) provides better coverage in some situations.

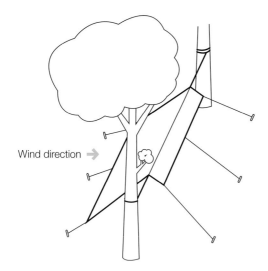

Wind direction →

Dining fly set up for cooking and eating in bad weather.

and eating areas should be unobstructed, but if you will be cooking over an open fire, you may wish to locate the eating area far enough from it so that smoke will not be bothersome.

Sanitation Area

Place the latrine at least 100 feet downwind from your tent and food areas, and 200 feet from any water source. It should be easy to get to from the tent, especially in the dark. If the path from tent to latrine is tricky, tie bits of cloth or string to bushes along the way to blaze the trail. Remember to remove these when breaking camp.

Avoiding living plants, dig a trench about 10 inches deep, and leave the displaced earth next to it, with a trowel or shovel handy. If campers are uncomfortable doing their business squatting, set up a leaning rail. Place a roll of toilet paper on a stake or branch and cover it with a plastic bag to keep it dry. After making a deposit, cover the waste with earth. Before leaving camp, replace the rest of the earth but do not pack it down tightly. Leaving it loosely packed allows oxygen-breathing microbes to break the waste down into harmless minerals.

Firewood Preparation Area

If you'll be building a fire, dedicate another area to the preparation of firewood. Some sites may already have a stump or wood block appropriate for splitting. If not, find an appropriate down tree that is clear of overhanging branches and anything else that could catch your axe on the backstroke. It should be far enough from the main centers of activity to eliminate danger to others from flying chips. Before extinguishing your last fire at the campsite, return the chopping area to its previous appearance by collecting and burning the accumulated chips and twigs. If you're in an established campsite, it's polite to leave a small amount of firewood and kindling near the fire ring, neatly piled and protected from rain for the next occupant.

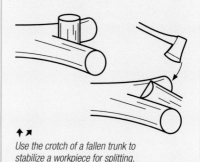

↑ ↗
Use the crotch of a fallen trunk to stabilize a workpiece for splitting.

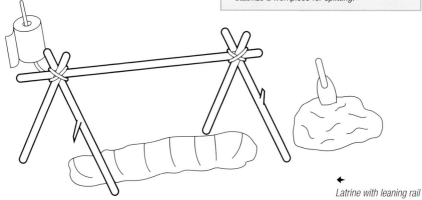

←
Latrine with leaning rail

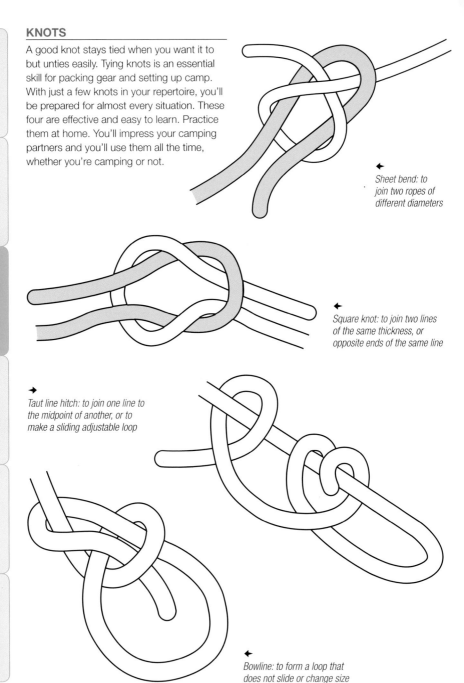

KNOTS

A good knot stays tied when you want it to but unties easily. Tying knots is an essential skill for packing gear and setting up camp. With just a few knots in your repertoire, you'll be prepared for almost every situation. These four are effective and easy to learn. Practice them at home. You'll impress your camping partners and you'll use them all the time, whether you're camping or not.

Sheet bend: to join two ropes of different diameters

Square knot: to join two lines of the same thickness, or opposite ends of the same line

Taut line hitch: to join one line to the midpoint of another, or to make a sliding adjustable loop

Bowline: to form a loop that does not slide or change size

Planning

Gear

Techniques

Hazards

Hiking

Camping with Kids

KEEPING FOOD SAFE

Animals large and small—from ants to bears—want a piece of your food supply. It's critical to deny them the pleasure, for your safety and theirs. (Bears who learn to raid campsites are more dangerous than those who avoid human contact, and land managers occasionally have to "dispose" of them.)

Never bring food into the tent. Even if you don't leave it there, the lingering odor of food may attract animals. Food must not be left in backpacks at ground level either, or you risk having them invaded by crawling insects, or torn up by animals with sharp claws or teeth.

Suspending food bags just 5 or 6 feet off the ground from a clothesline will suffice to keep them safe from ants, squirrels, mice, raccoons, skunks, and such. Make sure the bags are far enough from the supporting trees so that squirrels cannot jump onto them. If you're in bear country, food must be protected in a bearproof container, or by hanging a bear bag out of their reach.

Don't underestimate the intelligence of small mammals: they can and will open many ice chests. If yours lacks a secure latch, strap or tie it closed or pile pots and pans on the lid before retiring for the night. The noise they make knocking them over will frighten the animal away and alert you to the problem.

Avoid Foragers

Anything that smells like food might attract animals. In addition to food, keep items like toothpaste and antiperspirant sticks out of your tent.

Bear Bag

A bear bag should hang 12 to 15 feet off the ground, and 8 feet from the nearest tree. Some campers simply throw a rope over a branch, tie on the food bag and haul it up. If the bag is heavy, though, this will quickly wear out the rope and may damage the tree as well.

A good bear bag hoist consists of two strong but thin ropes and a small pulley. Tie the pulley to the end of one rope and throw it over a branch so that pulley is low enough to reach. Thread the second line through the pulley, then pull in on the first rope until the pulley is 14 to 18 feet high, taking care to keep hold of both ends of the second rope. (Tying them together temporarily makes this easy.)

Tie off the first rope to the tree trunk. Tie one end of the second rope to the food bag, and hoist away on the other end. Then tie that end to the tree trunk.

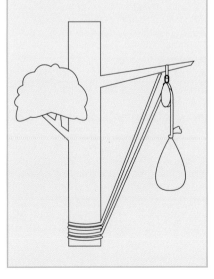

Planning

Gear

Techniques

Hazards

Hiking

Camping with Kids

Ice Chest Use

A good ice chest can keep food fresh as long as six days with regular (not dry) ice, but only if it's used properly:

- Keep it out of the sun, and out of a hot car
- Keep it closed as much as possible. Even a few extra seconds with the lid open makes a difference.
- Plan exactly what you need to make a meal before opening the cooler. When you're ready to open the chest, grab all the items you need in one go, and close it quickly.
- Melt water is nearly as cold as the ice itself. Don't drain melt water unless you have to to keep it from ruining food.

BREAKING CAMP

Moving out of a campsite should be done efficiently, with an eye toward returning it to the condition in which you originally found it—if not better.

Many campers repack their sleeping pads and bags before they even exit the tent in the morning. If everyone thus takes care of their personal gear, then one individual can take down the tent and work on other break-down jobs while others are preparing breakfast or washing up after it.

Repacking the Tent

After all gear has been removed from the tent, sweep out any dirt or grit. (A whisk broom is handy here.) Double-check the mesh pockets for forgotten items. Then close all window, screen, and flap zippers. Pull the stakes holding down the fly, then remove and collapse the poles. If the pole sections are connected by internal elastic cords, separate them first at the middle joint, then work your way out toward the ends. Remove the remaining stakes holding down the tent body. Count the stakes to make sure you have them all before placing them in their own little stuff sack.

If dew or rain fell overnight, dry the tent if possible by placing it in the sun. If it must be packed wet, take care to keep all that water on the outside. Don't stuff a wet tent. Lay the tent body flat; place the fly over it, wet-side up, then fold and roll it to fit into the stuff sack. As you roll it up, use your hand to sweep off any debris that sticks to the bottom of the floor.

Other Break-Down Tasks

Fire: Your fire must be completely out before you leave. If you want to get going early, make your morning fire a small one. Leave no charred wood or live coals: everything should be burnt down to ash.

Latrine: Fill in the latrine. Disassemble the leaning rail if you built one. Remove any blazes placed on the trail to the latrine or bathroom. Remember the toilet paper.

Stray stuff: Don't forget to collect the garbage bag, clothesline, bear-bag rigging and other items tied to trees, and the axe or saw tucked away in the wood-cutting area.

Sweep #1: After all gear has been packed, make a visual "sweep" of the entire campsite, looking for dropped trash, forgotten items, and anything that looks worse than when you arrived. Sweat the small stuff: pick up every bread-bag closure, bottle cap, twist-tie, and cigarette butt.

Sweep #2: This one's literal. Take a down branch and sweep the campsite of wood chips and footprints, and "fluff up" any trampled grass.

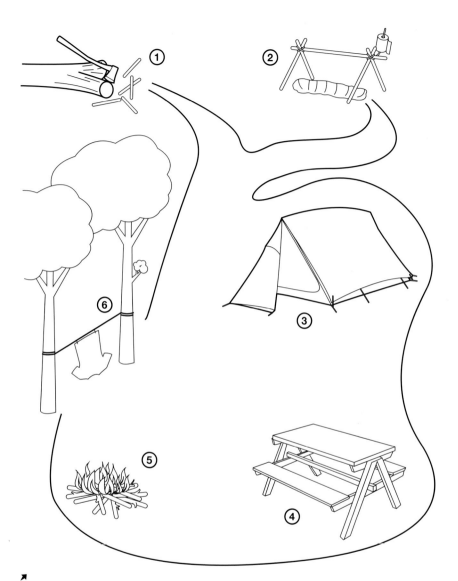

↗

When breaking camp, remember: (1) firewood prep area: retrieve axe, clean up chips and any cigarette butts; (2) latrine: retrieve toilet paper, break down leaning rail, fill pit; (3) tent: retrieve all gear, close zips, count stakes, brush off debris before stuffing; (4) eating area: clean up all trash and scraps; (5) fire pit: leave no charred wood or live coals, remove all trash; (6) trees: remove clothesline and anything else tied to trees.

Water

We rarely notice how much water we use when it's available at the tap. When we're camping, however, water consumption becomes an obvious and important consideration. Except for short trips of a day or two, you probably can't carry all the water you need, so you'll have to collect it as you go, and then make it safe to drink.

COLLECTING WATER

During vigorous physical activity in hot weather, your body may need as much as a quart of water every hour to replace what it loses through breathing, sweat, and urination. Over the course of a day, you may need nearly 2 gallons of water per person, plus additional for cooking. Even if not exercising, plan on a minimum of 2 quarts of water per person, per day.

As you plan your trip, look for water sources along your route. Topo maps may show only larger ones, but trail maps and guides are likely to include small streams and springs, and to give some indication about their reliability.

Some of these sources, though, may dry up seasonally or in dry years. When hiking in areas where water sources are few and far between, ask rangers or other knowledgeable sources just before you set out whether specific sources are flowing. Plan to carry enough water to take you from one source to the next, with some margin for error should a source prove unexpectedly dry.

Finding Water

If a stream or brook is dry, go downstream: there's a good chance that you'll find surface water. If that doesn't work, look for an area where streamside vegetation is healthy, and dig into the stream bed there. Or look for these hints:

Vegetation: In otherwise dry country, look for patches of vegetation or stands of trees. They're probably feeding off a water source, even if it's underground.

Cliffs: Water often seeps from between layers of exposed rock. The base of a cliff is a good place to look.

Valleys: If water is flowing from anywhere on a hill or mountain, no matter how little or how deep beneath the ground surface, it will eventually make its way downhill.

Animal signs: Follow animal tracks or the flight paths of bees or flies. They all need water and know where to find it.

Tips for Collecting Water

- Wide-mouth water bottles or cups work better than military-style canteens.
- If the source is too shallow to dip your bottle into, you may excavate the bottom to make it deeper. Wait several minutes for particles to settle before collecting.
- Alternatively, use a clean cloth to absorb water in shallow basins, then wring it out into a pan.

Planning

Gear

Techniques

Hazards

Hiking

Camping with Kids

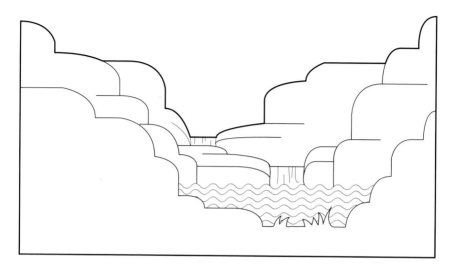

If the ground is even a bit moist, dig into it a foot or more and allow water to seep into the hole. In boggy or marshy ground, empty and discard the first water that fills this hole, because it will be full of sediment, then gently scoop out the second or third filling.

Following the contours of the land downhill will often lead you to a water source.

Collect Rainwater

Keep your containers as full as possible by collecting water whenever the opportunity presents itself. The next expected water source might prove to be dry.

Collecting rainwater is easy. Tie a plastic sheet or a tarp to bushes or trees and arrange it to funnel water into a pan or bottle. In areas without suitable tall vegetation, lay the tarp over a depression in the ground, then scoop up the collected water with a cup or soak it up with a clean rag and wring it into a pot before

transferring it into your water bottle. Rainwater is always drinkable, but if the tarp is dirty, you might need to filter it anyway.

Planning

Gear

Techniques

Hazards

Hiking

Camping with Kids

Producing Water

Even if water is unavailable from "regular" sources like streams and springs, you may be able to gather or produce enough to get by. Use a clean cloth to absorb dew from grass or other vegetation in the cool of the morning, wring it out, and repeat. Tie a clear plastic bag around the leaves at the end of a living tree branch. As the tree transpires, it will release moisture inside the bag.

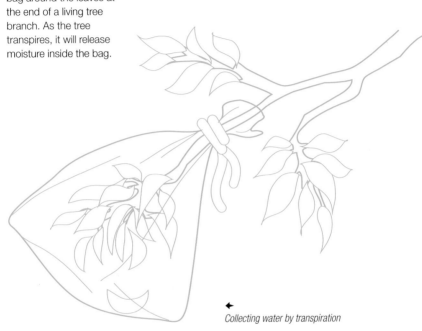

← Collecting water by transpiration

To gather more water from foliage, dig a large hole in the ground and place armfuls of fresh green leaves inside it. In the center of the hole, place a pan or other container. Cover the hole with a sheet of clear plastic and place dirt all around the edges of the plastic to seal the edges against the ground. Place a small stone in the center of the plastic sheet, directly above the container. As sunlight hits the plastic, heat will rise inside the hole. The leaves will give up their moisture, which will condense on the underside of the plastic, run down the slope, and drip into the container. Replace the leaves when they become thoroughly limp. This process will also work without leaves if there is moisture in the ground.

You can use a similar method to make salt water drinkable. Place a couple inches of salt water in a large container, and place a small cup in the middle with a clean stone inside it to prevent it from floating. Cover the container with a sheet of clear plastic, place a pebble in the center, and put the container in the sun. Water will evaporate, condense as pure, desalinated water on the underside of the plastic, and drip into the cup.

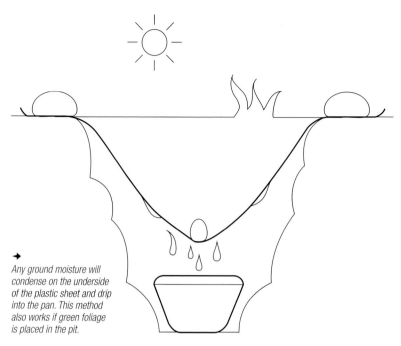

→ *Any ground moisture will condense on the underside of the plastic sheet and drip into the pan. This method also works if green foliage is placed in the pit.*

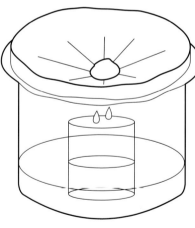

↗ *A salt-water still*

TREATING WATER

Water taken directly from a spring is likely to be safe. For any water taken from a surface source, such as a stream or lake, assume that it's contaminated and treat it accordingly.

Whether you use a filter, chemical treatment, or a UV device, always follow the instructions provided by the manufacturer. To purify water by boiling, you need only bring it to a vigorous rolling boil, then let it cool. Boiling for several minutes only wastes fuel and makes the water taste "flat."

Almost all water should first be coarsely filtered by running it through a piece of clean cloth, or perhaps a clean sock filled with sand. Even if you're using a mechanical filter device, this measure keeps out larger particles and so reduces the need to clean or replace the expensive filter element.

Planning

Gear

Techniques

Hazards

Hiking

Camping with Kids

Fire

Nothing typifies camping like a campfire. Many campers who do all their cooking over a stove still build a campfire at night. It's the hearth we gather around when the day's work and traveling are done. As we relax from the day's rigors, we stare into the flames and then the dying embers, telling stories, listening to night sounds, or just thinking about our place in the universe.

WHERE TO PUT IT

Land managers may impose specific rules for fires. Aside from regulating whether they are allowed at all, managers may require you to obtain a permit or to use only established fire rings or pits. In parts of the western U.S., fires may not be built directly on bare rock and a metal fire pan must be used to contain ashes and prevent long-term scars.

If selecting your own fire site, choose an area sheltered from the wind, clear of vegetation at least 5 feet in all directions, and with no overhanging branches. Scrape away loose twigs and leaves underfoot. Rock, sand, or mineral earth make a good base. Earth with a lot of decayed vegetable matter in it does not, as it can burn.

If you must build a fire in a grassy field, carefully remove a circle of sod with your entrenching tool, and place it safely several feet away. When you break camp, remove the stones from the fire ring and replace the sod.

Fire Enclosure

A fire ring contains the fire, concentrates its heat, and protects it from the wind. Use stones 6–10 inches across and don't make it too large: a ring of 12–16 inches inside diameter is big enough to cook a meal and warm a group of people, and small fires require less firewood. If stones are not available, build your fire between two parallel logs at least 6 inches in diameter and 10–12 inches apart. A floor of flat stones inside the enclosure will reflect heat and prevent moisture rising from the ground, which would cool the fire.

Don't build your fire enclosure from stones pulled from a river or lake. They have absorbed water that, when heated, will turn into steam that could cause them to explode.

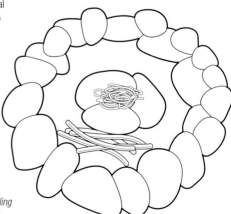

→ *Fire ring with a small floor of stones, and with kindling nearby, ready to add as soon as the tinder is alight.*

MATERIALS

Fires are built in three stages with three kinds of materials:

Tinder: Fine, dry, often fluffy material that is easy to light with a match, tinder provides the heat to light the kindling. Natural tinders include fibers stripped from weed stalks, fine dry grass, thistle down, dry moss, pine needles, dry leaves, and bird's nests. Birch bark and shredded cedar, palm, juniper, and sagebrush bark also work well, but should only be stripped from dead trees. Man-made tinders include paper, cotton balls, drier lint, jute string, and fire paste—a waxy substance that comes in a tube.

Kindling: Slightly larger material, consisting of twigs, cones, wood chips and shavings, and sticks ranging from toothpick size to pencil-thickness. Kindling provides the heat to light the fuel wood.

Fuel wood: This is what provides the heat to cook over, but burns slowly enough so that you don't have to constantly tend the fire. It's everything bigger than kindling, from finger-thickness sticks, to split sections of wood, to sawn branches and small logs.

Tinder and kindling must be perfectly dry. Some fuel wood can be damp on the outside, as long as it's not wet all the way through. Unless you're in a desert, any wood you find on the ground is probably too wet, if not rotten. Find dry materials by looking for dead trees that are still standing or supported by rocks or other trees. Branches that stick out from down trees may be dry, and some live trees may have dead branches low enough to reach.

Don't cut live trees or branches, and know the area's firewood management policy. Many areas prohibit the harvesting of dead wood from all standing trees, even if the tree itself is dead.

Until you've built several campfires, you'll be surprised at how much kindling and fuel wood you need. Gather twice as much as you expect to use, breaking lighter materials by hand, and using a knife, axe, or saw for splitting up the heavier stuff. Tinder may need to be picked apart or shredded; kindling broken and split, and fuel wood split, chopped, or sawn. Split logs burn better than whole logs of the same size.

Firewood Provisions

Drive-in campgrounds generally make for poor firewood collecting: they get so much traffic that any dead wood is quickly taken. Car-campers and RVers should bring their own firewood, or be prepared to buy a bundle at the campground store.

Planning

Gear

Techniques

Hazards

Hiking

Camping with Kids

BUILDING THE FIRE

Arrange your materials near the fire ring, with kindling and fuel wood sorted by size. Shove three sticks of kindling into the ground and angle them toward each other at the top so that they lean together. Then build a little kindling teepee, leaning more sticks against this tripod base. There should be 3 or 4 inches of open space inside, and an opening on one side.

Gather up a bunch of tinder and place it inside the teepee. Light it with a match and add more as it burns. As soon as the kindling begins to take fire, add more to the outside of the teepee. Keep adding kindling, in larger

and larger pieces, until the fire is big enough and hot enough to begin adding fuel wood. Again, start small and slowly work your way up to larger pieces. If some of your fuel wood is damp, lay it near the fire to begin drying it before placing it in the fire.

A good fire depends on a balance of fuel, heat, and oxygen. Place wood carefully onto the fire. If you just throw the wood on, the structure may collapse, restricting air circulation. When the pieces are the right distance from one another, they act like a well-designed fireplace, drawing heat and oxygen in at the base of the fire and funneling it up through the spaces between the sticks like a chimney. Too close, and they choke the circulation; too far, and the heat becomes too spread out, failing to keep the wood alight.

Add wood only when it's needed to maintain this delicate balance. Keep an eye on the fire, learn when to leave it alone, and don't build it larger than necessary. You want it to burn down to coals before you climb into your sleeping bag for the night, and you don't want to have to stay awake later than necessary. Neither do you want to extinguish it with water: that smells awful, makes clouds of unpleasant steam, and ruins the fire pit for the next day's use.

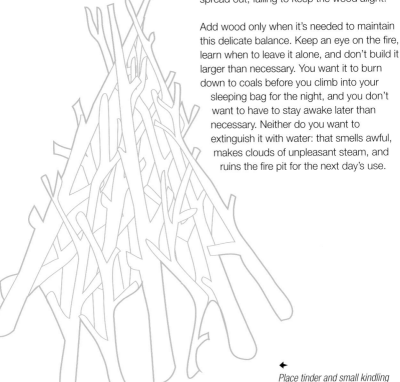

←
Place tinder and small kindling inside the "teepee" to start the fire.

Meals

Most backcountry campers value efficiency in meal preparation. In the morning, we're eager to hit the trail and start clicking off miles, and we don't want to spend time dawdling—especially if it's chilly. Lunch is essentially a refueling stop in the midst of the travels and typically involves no cooking at all. By suppertime, we're tired from a long, hard day. We want to replace lost calories and get everything cleaned up and put away before darkness falls.

PRE-TRIP FOOD PREPARATION

Much meal preparation can be done at home. Start with a detailed menu, listing every ingredient for each meal, including quantities. For multi-day trips, break it into separate lists, and include preparation instructions beside each item. Store the lists in a zip-lock bag, and pack it with your cooking kit. Keep records of every trip: what you ate, how much you had, whether it was enough, whether you enjoyed it. After a few trips, you'll be able to assemble a trip menu easily and quickly by referring to your records.

Use the detailed list, including quantities, as the basis of your shopping list. After you've brought the food home, get rid of every bit of excess packaging: throw out cardboard boxes and put dry foods in zip-lock bags. Measure and pre-mix all the dry ingredients for each dish into bags. Put all the elements for a single meal into a "meal bag," then distribute the meal bags into "day bags," each containing breakfast, lunch, and supper for a single day. Use another bag for items needed for many meals: cooking oil, sugar, coffee, tea, salt, etc.

Many experienced campers don't plan specific lunch menus. Instead, another bag holds all the lunch goods, and campers choose whatever they feel like. Common options include peanut butter, preserves, durable cheese, crackers, wraps, dried fruit, hard salami, summer sausage, jerky, canned sardines, cooked bacon (either left over from breakfast or in shelf-stable packaging), granola bars, and gorp.

Dehydrating Food

Dehydrators make it possible to bring foods that would otherwise spoil, or be too heavy or bulky to carry. Dried fruit and fruit leathers have almost the same nutritional value as fresh fruit, but at a fraction of the weight and volume. Fresh mushrooms don't travel well, but dried, they're fine. Tomato sauce can be dried into a leather and reconstituted in camp by soaking and simmering. Some other foods that can be successfully dehydrated for camping include:

- apples
- pears
- peaches
- pineapple
- blueberries
- onions
- peppers
- salsa
- tomatoes (including cherry tomatoes)
- broccoli
- cauliflower
- potatoes
- pickle slices
- canned fruits and vegetables (pineapple, peaches, beans, etc.)
- frozen vegetables (corn, peas, mixed veggies, etc.)

Pre-Wash Food

Wash fresh produce at home to save time and conserve water when camping.

Planning

Gear

Techniques

Hazards

Hiking

Camping with Kids

Prepping the Ice Chest

A good ice chest will keep food cold for five or six days if you know how to use it. Used incorrectly, your ice might be gone in a day or two. Here's the right way:

- Use only block ice. It's *all* ice. A bag of cube or crushed ice is almost half air.
- Make your own block ice in plastic ½-gallon or 1-gallon milk jugs. This is cheaper, and the jugs will contain the melt water, keeping the ice colder and preventing it from soaking your food.
- Freeze all food that can be frozen.
- A day or two before you pack, chill the food as much as possible by turning your freezer and refrigerator to their coldest settings.
- Pre-cool the ice chest by placing several ice blocks in it for 6 to 8 hours before you load it.
- When you're ready to load the food, replace the blocks that were used to pre-cool the chest with colder ones right out of the freezer.

COOKING ON A STOVE

Every camping stove manufacturer provides adequate instructions for lighting and maintaining the stove, refueling it, turning it off, and regulating the flame. Read these carefully and follow them closely. Practice running the stove at home before your first camping trip.

Most backpacker stoves do not provide an especially stable base for cooking pots. Minimize these problems by placing the stove on a solid surface, making sure it's perfectly level, and avoiding pots that are larger than necessary. When stirring a pot, hold it securely with a pot holder or gripper, or remove it briefly from the stove and place it on a stable surface to stir the contents.

Some stoves are less affected by wind than others, but almost all will perform better if shielded from the breeze by placing them

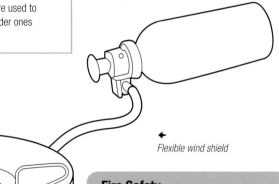

Flexible wind shield

Fire Safety

Camping stoves are potentially dangerous and must be used with care. All camping stoves generate deadly carbon monoxide gas, and liquid-fuel stoves can flare up unexpectedly. Never use them in an enclosed space like an RV or a tent.

behind a large rock or inside a fire ring. A flexible metal shield that encloses the stove and wraps closely around the cooking pot protects the flame from wind and ensures that most of the stove's heat is directed toward the bottom of the pot, thus reducing cooking time and fuel consumption.

COOKING ON A CAMPFIRE

Cooking is easier and safer over a low, steady flame. After lighting and building up the fire, wait for the flames to die down a bit before starting to cook.

Fire rings in many established campsites have heavy steel grates. These are intended to support cooking pots, not to be cooked on directly in the manner of a barbecue grill. Unfortunately, the grates are often too high to cook on efficiently. To deal with this, three approaches work better than building a bigger fire:

- If the grate can be tilted or shifted out of the way: Place three rocks in a triangle inside the fire ring, and build a small fire within the triangle. The rocks serve as a tripod on which to set your cooking pot.
- Bring your own fire grate. A grate can be borrowed from your oven or toaster oven at home. Grates for backpackers weigh just a few ounces and some have folding legs designed to support the grate at a reasonable height. If there are no legs, support it on stones.
- If the grate can't be shifted, wait until the fire dies down to coals, then place the pot beneath the grate, directly on the coals. Cooking on coals is a good strategy in any case.

One of the drawbacks of cooking on a campfire is that the pots become covered with soot. Cooking directly on coals, instead of live flame, reduces this problem. Rubbing the outside of the pot with bar soap before cooking prevents soot from sticking and makes pots easier to clean. But neither of these measures is completely effective, so carry your pots in a plastic or cloth bag to avoid transferring soot to other gear.

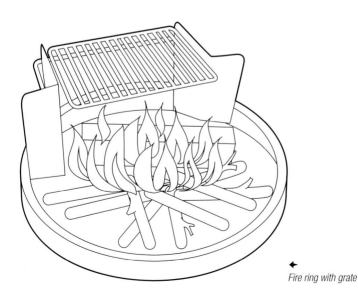

← Fire ring with grate

Planning

Gear

Techniques

Hazards

Hiking

Camping with Kids

Using a Dutch Oven

A Dutch oven is a versatile pot that can be used for baking, boiling, simmering, sautéing, roasting, and stewing. True Dutch ovens are cast with stubby tripod legs to hold them just above the cooking coals. The lid is recessed to hold coals on top and thus provide heat all around—essential for baking. While cast-iron ovens are too heavy for anything but car-camping or boat camping, aluminum versions are light enough for short backpacking trips.

One of the advantages of Dutch ovens is that they allow good temperature control for baking when used with charcoal briquettes. (The coals are ready to use when they become lightly covered with white ash.) Placing eight briquettes on the lid and four below the pot will maintain a steady 250–300°F in a 10 inch-diameter oven. Use ten briquettes on top and four below for 300–350°F, and twelve on top and five below for 350–400°F. Increase these numbers by half if using a 12 inch pot. Wood coals may be used in place of briquettes, but temperature control will be less predictable.

When baking in a Dutch oven, it's essential to keep the lid on and trust the recipe for the correct amount of time. Open it for just a second to look, and you will lose your baking heat. If you can hear the food popping and sizzling, it's too hot. To cool it down, take the pot from the fire for a couple minutes and remove about a quarter of the coals, top and bottom, before replacing it.

Minimize Clean-Up

Much cooking can be done in aluminum foil, which weighs little, need not be washed, and can be packed out. Store used foil in an airtight container to avoid attracting animals. Paper plates can be burned, but these are viable only for car-campers or very short human-powered trips where their weight and volume remain low.

Another approach is to use non-stick cookware, and spray it with window cleaner as soon as the food is dished up. After eating, wipe it clean with paper towels and rinse in clean water. Burn or pack out the towels.

CLEAN-UP

A proper after-meal clean-up accomplishes—and prevents—many things. It ensures that the cookware and eating utensils are sanitary. It prevents food trash from attracting animal pests. And it avoids polluting the environment.

As soon as the food has been dished up, fill the cooking pot with water and begin heating it. Remove it from the stove or fire when the water is too hot to stick your hand in: it'll cool while eat your meal. Add a few drops of biodegradable soap. This is your wash pot, and by heating water in it, you've already begun to soften cooked-on food.

For the hot rinse, heat another pot of water and add a tablespoon of bleach or other disinfectant. For the cold rinse, fill a third container with cold water that has been filtered or is otherwise suitable for drinking. (You need not use drinkable water in the first two pots if you bring it to boiling point first.)

Scrape all food scraps from dishes into a trash container, then put the dishes in the wash pot and scrub off all remaining food and grease. Next, holding them with tongs, dip each item into the hot rinse, remove, drain, then swish them around in the cold rinse. Allow everything to air-dry on a clean cloth, or by hanging it all in a net bag.

Empty the cold rinse water. Scrub the inside of the wash pot, then pour the wash water through a strainer into the cold-rinse bucket. Transfer food scraps from the strainer into your trash container. Pour the hot-rinse water first into the wash pot, then into the cold-rinse bucket to disinfect them, then dispose of all remaining water by tossing it over a broad area at least 200 feet from a water source. Don't pour it into the outhouse toilet.

MENU PLANNING

Car-campers and RVers have a great deal of flexibility in their menus: they can carry heavy and bulky foods and cooking gear, bring a cooler for perishables, and drive into town to restock whenever they want. Backpackers, boat campers, and backcountry bicyclists all need to plan more carefully, considering weight, bulk, nutritional value, and ease of preparation and clean-up. Make sure you have enough variety to keep it interesting, but don't be afraid to duplicate a meal or two during a multi-day trip. The following list consists of easy-to-prepare dishes that many campers swear by, but there are no limits to the number of appropriate choices.

Menu Suggestions

Breakfasts	Lunches	Suppers
• Hot cereals (oatmeal, polenta, cream of wheat) • Cold cereals (granola, muesli; use powdered milk if hiking or biking) • Breakfast burritos • Egg-scrambles (powdered eggs with any of the following mixed in: fried potatoes, onions, mushrooms, tomatoes, bacon bits, sausage, cheese) • French toast (use powdered eggs) • Biscuits with butter/ margarine, syrup/honey/ preserves • Pancakes • Bannock (a quick camping bread) • Corn bread • Rice and… (beans, cheese, fruit preserves; use leftover rice from previous supper) • Toasted cheese sandwiches	• Bagels or wraps (with peanut butter, preserves, cheese, humus) • Leftover breakfast breads (bannock, corn bread, biscuits, pancakes) • Grab-bag (gorp, dried fruit, hard candy, fruit leather, pumpkin and sunflower seeds) • Energy bars, granola bars • Canned sardines, kippers • Hard salami, summer sausage • Jerky A few easy-cooking choices: • Quesadillas • Instant soup • Toasted cheese sandwiches	*Most of the following are one-pot meals for ease of preparation and clean-up:* • Stews and soups • Macaroni and cheese • Spaghetti and sauce (tomato, pesto, Alfredo, garlic and oil, etc.) • Lo mein with peanut sauce and vegetables • Casseroles • Tacos, burritos, enchiladas, fajitas • Frittatas • Polenta with cheese and sausage • Shepherd's pie • Chicken and dumplings • Chicken cacciatore • Rice and beans • Curried vegetables and rice • Foil-baked fish, chicken, chops, potatoes • Pizza

Planning

Gear

Techniques

Hazards

Hiking

Camping with Kids

Recipes

Dozens of resources claim to provide gourmet recipes for backpackers and other backwoods campers. By "gourmet," most of their authors seem to mean "not totally bland and boring." That's OK, because most are satisfied with wholesome and filling, and no one has ever complained about the lack of French names, "presentation," or subtlety. These simple breakfast and supper dishes should provide enough interest and variety, but by all means get fancier if you're so inclined.

BREAKFASTS

Cinnamon Rolls

Ingredients
- 3 cups biscuit mix
- 2 tbsp. flour for rolling
- 6 tbsp. margarine or softened butter
- ½ cup brown sugar
- 1 tbsp. cinnamon
- ¼ cup raisins

Serves 4.

At home
Combine sugar, cinnamon, raisins in a zip-lock bag.

Preparation
Mix ¼ cup water into biscuit mix to form dough. Powder a flat surface (like a canoe bottom or wax-paper-covered table). Roll the dough to ¼ inch thickness and 10–12 inches wide. Spread 4 tbsp. margarine on the dough, then add the sugar mixture on top. Roll into a log, then cut into 1-inch slices. Use remaining margarine to grease the inside of a Dutch oven. Lay slices flat in oven, touching each other. Cover and bake over low heat for 9–10 minutes. (Can also be baked in reflector oven.)

Cheese Grits

Ingredients
- 1 cup quick corn grits (not instant)
- 1 tsp. salt
- 4 tbsp. powdered egg (or two fresh eggs)
- 6 tbsp. margarine or butter
- 1 cup grated cheddar, Parmesan, or Gouda cheese
- 8 oz. crumbled bacon

Serves 2.

At home
Combine grits and salt in a zip-lock bag.

Preparation
Stir grits and salt into 4 cups boiling water. Cook until thick, remove from heat and transfer into a bowl. If using powdered eggs, mix with ½ cup water. Stir in eggs, 5 tbsp. margarine, bacon, cheese. Grease Dutch oven with remaining margarine. Add grits mixture, cover, and bake at medium heat for 20 minutes. (Can also be cooked in open, ungreased pot: add ¾ cup additional water and simmer until thick.)

Skillet Potatoes

Ingredients
- ½ cup dried green pepper
- 4 medium potatoes
- 8 oz. sausage
- small onion
- 2 tbsp. cooking oil
- 1 tsp. thyme
- 4 oz. cheese (cheddar or other), cubed or grated

Serves 4.

At home
None.

Preparation
Soak peppers until plump, then remove from water. Cut potatoes into 1-inch cubes, place in water, and boil 5–10 minutes until nearly soft. Drain and set aside with peppers. Cut sausage into bite-sizes, and chop onion. Heat oil in fry pan and cook sausages and onion until sausages are nearly done. Add potatoes, peppers, spices. Cook over medium-high heat until potatoes are browned. Add cheese, heat until melted, and serve.

Really Good Oatmeal

Ingredients
- 2 cups rolled (not quick) oats (or 1 cup steel-cut oats)
- ½ cup raisins, currants, or dried cranberries
- 2 tbsp. brown sugar (or 3 tbsp. real maple syrup)
- ¼ cup walnuts

Serves 2.

At home
None.

Preparation
For rolled oats, bring 4 cups water to a boil, add oats, and cook for 5 minutes. (For steel-cut oats, boil 3 cups water and cook 15 minutes.) Add dried fruit and cook another 3–4 minutes, stirring occasionally. Serve with sugar and walnuts.

Alternative preparations
Oatmeal is a great camping food: it's light, nutritious, and so versatile that you can have it several breakfasts in a row without getting bored. Try adding diced apricots or prunes, dried (and revived) blueberries, sliced or slivered almonds, sunflower or pumpkin seeds. Or skip the sweets and try a savory approach, adding any of the following: thyme, rosemary, salt, pepper, sesame or poppy seeds, bacon crumbles, sausage, grated Parmesan or Gruyère cheese. Another option: allow it to cool, cut it into slices, and fry it, serving with either sweet or savory accompaniments.

Polenta with Bacon

Ingredients
- 1 cup polenta (coarse corn grits), dry
- 4 tbsp. crumbled bacon (shelf-stable or cooked)
- 1 tbsp. onion flakes
- 4 tsp. margarine
- 2 tsp. chicken or vegetable broth powder
- ½ tsp. paprika
- 1 cup Parmesan cheese

Serves 2.

At home
Everything except the cheese may be combined and packed in a zip-lock bag.

Preparation
Bring 3 cups water to a boil. Add all ingredients except the cheese; simmer until cooked and creamy. Top with the cheese.

Tuna or Chicken with Couscous

Ingredients
- ⅔ cup couscous (plain or flavored)
- 4 tbsp. dried mixed vegetables
- additional seasonings to taste
- 1 vacuum-sealed pouch of tuna or chicken (6–7 oz.)

Serves 2.

At home
Combine all ingredients except meat in a zip-lock bag.

Preparation
Boil 1⅓ cups water. Add dry ingredients and stir. Add meat and mix in. Let sit for 5 minutes to absorb water.

Lemony-Garlicky Pasta

Ingredients
- 6 tbsp. olive oil
- 2 tbsp. lemon juice
- 2 tsp. oregano and/or basil
- 2 garlic cloves, minced (or garlic power)
- 12 oz. pasta
- ⅛ cup Parmesan cheese
- salt, pepper to taste

Serves 2.

At home
Combine all ingredients except pasta and cheese in a small, oilproof food container. If using long pasta like spaghetti, break it in half and pack it in a zip-lock bag.

Preparation
Boil water and cook pasta 5–10 minutes. Strain liquid. Mix in lemon-garlic oil and half the cheese. Place in bowls and sprinkle with remaining cheese.

Curried Chicken and Rice

Ingredients
- 1 vacuum-sealed pouch of chicken (6-7 oz.)
- 1 tbsp. dried cilantro
- 1 tbsp. curry power
- 1 cup quick-cooking rice
- 4 flatbread wraps, pita, or tortillas

Serves 2.

At home
Combine rice and spices in a zip-lock bag.

Preparation
Place chicken in a pot with ⅔ cup water. Bring to a boil. Remove chicken, add cilantro and boil for 2 more minutes. Add curry powder and rice. Stir, cover, remove from heat. While rice absorbs water, dice chicken and mix it in. Re-cover, wait 5 minutes, then serve with flatbread.

Roughing It Stew

Ingredients
- 1 lb. beef jerky
- 7–8 dried tomatoes
- 1 large potato
- 1 large carrot
- 1 medium onion
- ¼ cup dried green peppers
- ¼ cup flour

Serves 4.

At home
Wash the fresh vegetables to save water on the trail.

Preparation
Chop up jerky and place in pot with 6 cups water. After boiling 15–20 minutes, add dried tomatoes. Chop potato, carrot, and onion and add, along with peppers. Cover and cook 30 minutes. When vegetables and beef are nearly soft enough, slowly add flour and stir in until desired thickness is achieved.

Alternative preparations
This recipe uses no seasonings because most jerky is highly spiced, but if you're using a mild jerky, add 1 tsp. garlic powder, 2 bay leaves, 2 tsp. dried basil or oregano, black pepper to taste. Dried black or white beans may be added at the start. Dried mushrooms may be added with the tomatoes. Instead of thickening with flour, add ½ cup bulgur wheat and additional ½ cup of water 15 minutes after vegetables are added.

Chicken and Dumplings

Ingredients
- 6 oz. biscuit mix
- 4 tbsp. corn starch
- ¾ cup dried celery
- ¾ cup dried carrots
- 2 bay leaves
- 5 chicken bouillon cubes
- ¼ tsp. poultry seasoning
- 1 vacuum-sealed pouch of chicken (6–7 oz.)
- salt, pepper to taste

Serves 2–3.

At home
Combine celery, carrots, bay leaves, bouillon cubes, poultry seasoning in a zip-lock bag.

Preparation
Stir ½ cup water into biscuit mix and set aside. Slowly add corn starch to 5 cups water and stir until smooth. Add vegetable and seasoning mixture. Bring to a boil, then simmer 5 minutes. Add chicken. Drop large dollops of biscuit dough on top of stew. (Don't stir them in!) Cover and cook 5–10 minutes, until dumplings are cooked through.

Planning

Gear

Techniques

Hazards

Hiking

Camping with Kids

Weather

At a particular canoe symposium, a wise saying is repeated every year: There is no bad weather, only inappropriate clothing choices. Sure, you might have the option of bailing out of your trip or staying in your RV and watching movies until the sun shines. But if you view the weather as an integral part of the outdoor experience, and you prepare yourself properly, it's possible to carry on in spite of rain, cold, or extreme heat and still enjoy yourself.

FORECASTING...MAYBE NOT

Many camping books spend pages explaining weather dynamics and how to read weather maps. Of course, if you had access to current weather maps, you'd also have access to current weather reports generated by professional meteorologists! As for observing the movements of animals, red skies at morning and other such folk wisdom —well, you never hear a meteorologist using that information to make or support a forecast.

The best resource for weather information is a weather-band radio that picks up nonstop local reports from the National Weather Service. Otherwise, stay alert to these easily observed natural signs:

Cold front: If the wind suddenly rises or shifts and the temperature drops significantly along with it, a cold front is moving in. Aside from the fact that the cold might be of long duration, it can cause heavy rainfall.

Line squall: If you're in flat, open country, and you see a low, dark wall of clouds moving toward you, you're observing a heavy rainstorm accompanying the leading edge of a front. Take shelter fast.

Cumulonimbus clouds: These are huge, dark, towering clouds with an "anvil-shaped" top. Expect a thunderstorm.

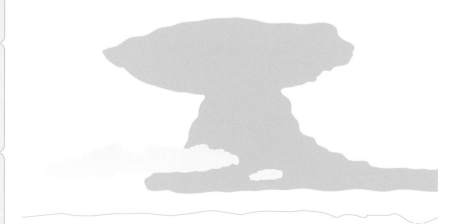

↑
A cumulonimbus cloud

WEATHER PREPAREDNESS

No matter where or when you camp, you should always be prepared for the coldest or worst weather known to occur during that time of year. This applies to the gear you bring on your trip and, to a lesser extent, to the gear you have with you at any given moment. Should you leave camp for a day-hike, carry a daypack containing extra clothing for any change in weather that might occur.

Regulating Heat

This is especially true if your day-hike will take you to a higher elevation, and especially again if you'll walk above the treeline. Temperature drops rapidly with elevation, and if there are no trees to break the wind, you'll be doubly exposed. Even in the height of summer, never walk above the treeline without having long trousers, a weatherproof outer garment and a hat in your daypack.

Whether hiking, biking, or boating, pack your gear so that you can grab and shed protection quickly and easily. Vigorous exercise generates heat and sweat, and after just a few minutes of hiking, you might need to strip off some outerwear, even in cool weather. However, as soon as you stop, be ready to put some on to maintain body heat.

STAY DRY TO STAY WARM

All by itself, getting wet is no big deal. It's water's capacity to suck heat out of our bodies that makes it so important to stay dry in anything but the warmest weather. A full suit of raingear with a full-coverage hood or a large-brimmed rain hat should be near the top of your pack.

When entering your tent, avoid bringing water in with you, for a wet sleeping bag is a miserable thing. Strip off your raingear in the vestibule if your tent has one. If not, push your sleeping bag and other dry gear to the opposite end of the tent and sit just inside the door with your feet outside. Take off your boots and place them outside the tent, beneath the fly. Remove your raingear carefully, roll it up to keep the water on the outside, and place it on a plastic bag just inside the door. Wipe up any water on the tent floor before rearranging your sleeping bag.

It's difficult to stay dry while cooking and eating if you don't have a kitchen fly. You might choose to subsist on food that requires no cooking while the storm lasts, but to avoid attracting animal pests, don't bring food into the tent.

The Right Hat

A knit or fleece hat is the best and most effective way to quickly regulate body temperature. In cold weather, a hat will keep your head warm and help it to stay nice and dry.

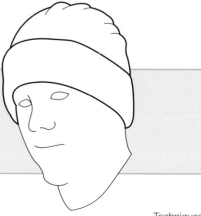

Planning

Gear

Techniques

Hazards

Hiking

Camping with Kids

On the Move in Cold and Wet

Pay attention to your stomach when hiking or biking in cold, wet weather. Don't wait until you're hungry or thirsty: replace lost energy by snacking often on high-carbohydrate foods like gorp or energy bars, and stay hydrated by drinking small amounts of water frequently.

When you're cold, stop. If your current level of exercise isn't keeping you warm, then expending even more calories will only make you colder. Warm yourself by putting on extra layers, boiling water for a hot drink, or even setting up the tent and crawling into the sleeping bag. Get warm before proceeding, or stay where you are. An inconvenient campsite is better than hypothermia.

HOT WEATHER COMFORT

Hot weather entails risks too. Here are some ways to stay comfortable and safe when the mercury soars:

Stay Hydrated

Drink water often and in large volumes.

Replace Lost Salts

Heavy sweating causes a loss of minerals needed for good health. These can be replaced with powdered electrolyte mixes that are available to add to water. Other options include salt tablets and salty foods.

Keep Yourself Wet

Whenever you have a chance, take a dip in a stream. If the water source is too shallow to bathe, dip your bandana, wipe yourself down, then re-dip it and tie it around your neck. Soak your hat and shirt as well.

Lightning Safety

Lightning can surely kill you. Thunder follows lightning, and sound travels about a mile in five seconds. That's considered the danger zone. If you see a flash, then hear thunder within five seconds, you should take shelter. Of course that's not foolproof. Storms can move quickly and extend for miles. The last strike might have been two miles away; the next one might be right over you.

Avoid being, or sheltering under, the tallest thing in the neighborhood. Boats are inevitably the highest thing on a body of water, so if you're in one, head for shore and stay there for 30 minutes following the last lightning. Woods are generally safe, but shelter beneath lower trees and away from the forest giants.

If you're caught in a lightning storm on open ground with no shelter available, roll out your foam sleeping pad and use it to insulate yourself from the ground. Squat, don't sit, on the pad to lower your height and minimize the area of contact. In rocky, treeless areas, avoid depressions that collect water that could attract ground lightning.

Rest

During the afternoon—the hottest part of the day—find a shady place and take a rest. "Losing" a couple of hours is okay, because the sun stays up longer in summer, so you can continue your travels later in the day. If natural shade isn't available, set up your tent fly. Don't bother with the tent body, because it will restrict air flow.

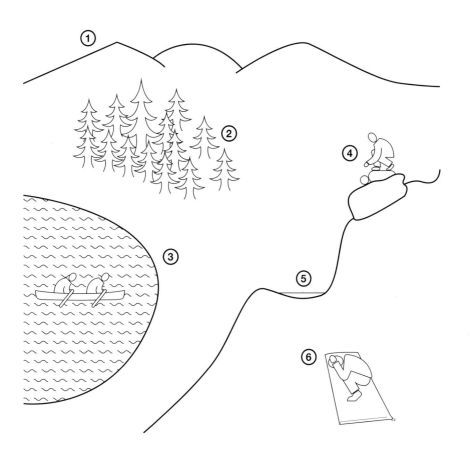

↑

Lightning safety: (1) avoid high, bare ground; (2) shelter beneath low trees, avoid the tallest; (3) get off the water; (4) on exposed ground, place backpack on a boulder and squat on it; (5) avoid low spots on exposed ground where water collects; (6) squat on foam sleeping pad.

Tornadoes

Tornadoes are common in some regions during certain seasons, but can occur almost anywhere at any time. Most are quickly observed and reported, so weather radios provide good early warning. If one approaches, get out of your car, RV, or tent and seek secure shelter in a ditch or at the base of a solid rock wall or large boulder.

4 HAZARDS

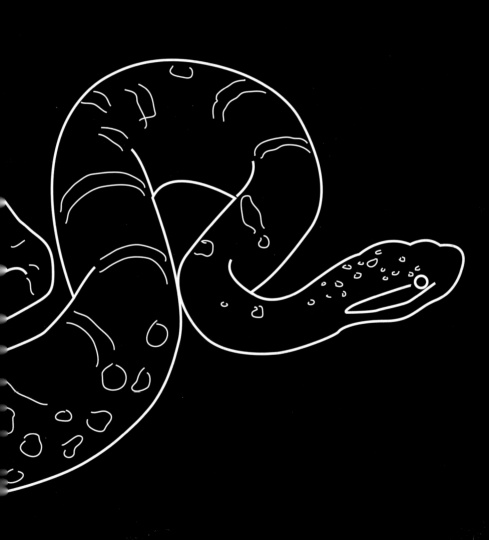

Dangerous and Nuisance Animals

Planning

While encounters with nuisance animals are common and almost to be expected in many areas, run-ins with truly dangerous animals are rare in the United States. Novice campers tend to worry a lot about the potentially deadly beasts, when mosquitoes are much more likely to be a problem. Not that we should ignore the potential dangers of "nature red in tooth and claw," but neither should they keep us from enjoying the outdoors with a justified feeling of safety and confidence.

MAMMALS

We'll address mammals first because they seem to be the greatest fear of inexperienced campers. We hope that a little familiarity will change that.

Bears

Black bears are quite timid and can usually be scared away just by making them think you're a threat. This isn't difficult. Stand tall, wave your arms, make a lot of noise by yelling or banging pans together, and throw rocks or sticks. Keep them out of your campsite by securing your food (see page 93) and they'll likely leave you alone.

The only situations in which a black bear is likely to attack is if you surprise it at close range or appear to be threatening a sow's cub. When hiking through dense woods where sight lines are restricted, attach a set of bear bells (available from outfitters) to your backpack. The tinkling sound will alert any bears up ahead of your approach, and they'll be gone before you know they were there.

Grizzly or brown bears can be more aggressive and may not be deterred by a show of strength on your part. Avoid hiking alone in grizzly territory, use bear bells, and remain alert to signs of bear on the trail: clawed bark on tree trunks, and paw prints and *scat* (feces) on the trail. Be scrupulous about keeping yourself and your tent free of meat odors and sweet smells that may signal food, including many cosmetics. Even clothing that has absorbed food odors should be kept outside the tent.

Black bear with paw print

Grizzly bear with paw print

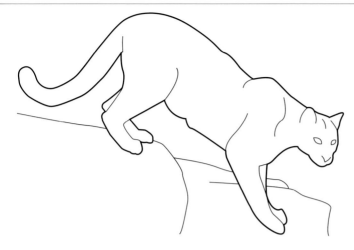

Mountain lion

You can't outrun a grizzly bear, regardless of the terrain. A can of aerosol bear repellent is the best way to fend off a threatening bear, and if you're in grizzly country, you should carry a can ready to use in a belt holster. If you are attacked, don't think about fighting back: the more you fight, the worse you'll come off. Instead, lie prone, allow your backpack to protect your back, and absorb the punishment. Eventually the bear will decide that you're no longer a threat and leave you alone. She doesn't plan to eat you: at least you can get that off your mind.

Mountain Lions and Other Large Mammals

There have been only about 50 deaths by mountain lion (also known as cougar, puma, and catamount) in the past 100 years, and about half of those were young children unaccompanied by adults. In the highly unlikely event that you're threatened, don't run. First, you can't outrun an animal that earns its living chasing down deer. Second, that's what prey does, and you don't want to look like prey because, unlike grizzly bears, cougars may indeed make a meal of you.

Instead, make yourself appear threatening like the apex predator you are. Stand tall, look the cat in the eyes, shout, hold your arms wide or open your jacket and spread it wide to make yourself look bigger. Throw things, but only if you can reach them without bending down and looking small and vulnerable. If attacked, fight back with rocks, sticks, a fishing pole, or whatever else is at hand.

Owners should but don't always keep control of their dogs in public areas. Most seemingly aggressive dogs are actually defending their perceived territory: as long as you don't push forward, they won't attack. If the dog clearly belongs to someone, yell until the owner responds to take control. Appearing large and threatening will almost always prevent an attack, but if one seems inevitable, fighting back is the recommended response. Bear repellent is also effective.

Concerning dogs' near cousins, wolves: don't worry about them. There are a total of two documented instances of people being killed by wolves in North America.

Planning

Gear

Techniques

Hazards

Hiking

Camping with Kids

Nuisance Mammals

Squirrels, chipmunks, raccoons, and rodents are by far the most likely mammals to cause problems to campers, but only because they steal food and chew through food packs to get to it. The problem is easily avoided by following proper food storage procedures (see page 93).

Skunks, of course, should be avoided. If you encounter one on the trail, just get out of its way and let it pass. If one passes through your campsite, stay cool and let it go. The only reason it may stick around is if you left food unguarded. You really don't want to risk the consequences of trying to scare it off.

Unless it's rabid, no other North American mammal represents a danger unless you determinedly interfere with it. Leave porcupines, raccoons, foxes, beavers, woodchucks, etc., alone, and you'll be fine. Mess with them, and they'll scratch and bite viciously.

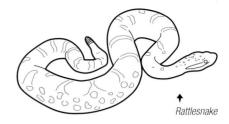

Rattlesnake

REPTILES

With the rare exception of alligators and crocodiles, it is reassuring to know that no reptile will ever stalk or bite you, unless you threaten it or step on it accidentally.

The rattlesnake is the deadliest of America's venomous snakes, and even their bites result in death less than $\frac{1}{10}$ of 1 percent of the time. The other dangerous snakes are copperheads, coral snakes, and water moccasins (also known as cottonmouths). While you certainly don't want to get bitten, none of them are quite as fearsome as their reputations.

Nonetheless, avoidance is the only sensible policy. If you encounter one in the open, give it wide berth. When scrambling around boulders or fallen logs, remain alert to their presence. The effectiveness of commercial snake-bite kits, including venom extractors, is highly questionable, and the only sure treatment is an injection of the appropriate antivenin.

Alligators and crocodiles are ambush hunters: they wait in hiding for prey to pass within close range—generally close enough to grab with a single lunge. Neither will chase you on land, but really large ones might pursue you in water. Avoidance of their habitats, and maintaining a high level of awareness when avoidance is not possible, are the appropriate safety measures.

Snapping turtles are a danger only because so many people thoughtlessly interfere with them. They can bite off a finger, but only if you invite them to do so.

Rabies

Assume that any mammal that behaves in a truly bizarre manner could be rabid. In addition to the well-known (but not always present) foaming at the mouth, indicators include snapping at nothing, walking unsteadily, the appearance of choking, and twisting in circles. Nocturnal animals like raccoons and foxes who are abroad in full daylight should be suspect, as should any animal that normally avoids people but that approaches you in a seemingly friendly way. Avoid all such mammals if possible. If they approach, chase them off by throwing rocks or swinging sticks at them.

INSECTS AND SUCH

The animals that are by far the most likely to create unpleasantness to campers are arthropods—buggy things with jointed legs, segmented bodies, and exoskeletons, including insects, arachnids (e.g., spiders and ticks), and centipedes.

Mosquitoes

The bane of eastern and southern campers, mosquitoes are not a problem in western mountains and deserts. Depending upon the season and the locale, they may be entirely absent, a minor inconvenience, or a maddening horror. They are also profligate vectors of disease, so even if you'd otherwise be willing to put up with the inconvenience, you should still take all reasonable measures to keep them off.

Where mosquito concentrations are low or moderate, personal insect repellent containing DEET is effective. In still weather and when sitting still, as in during meals, burning citronella candles or mosquito coils will help keep them outside of a small radius.

Where mosquitoes are truly bad, it's necessary to supplement the chemical warfare with a physical barrier. Wear bug suits and head nets when out of the tent. Eating with a headnet is awkward but may be necessary. For car campers and boat campers, a screen house makes a nice refuge for eating and relaxing. When entering and exiting tents, brush the mosquitoes from your clothes, shake the door screen to momentarily chase the pests off, then unzip, pass through, and rezip, all as quickly as possible. Spend a few minutes chasing down any that enter with you.

Insect Repellent

Most commercial insect repellents for personal application rely on the chemical DEET (N,N-Diethyl-meta-toluamide), available in concentrations from 10 percent to 100 percent. Research suggests that concentrations higher than 40 percent may not be more effective at repelling insects, but that higher concentrations do provide longer-lasting protection. It is available in liquid and spray form.

Rules for safe, effective DEET usage:

- Avoid eyes, nostrils, mouth, and mucous membranes. If accidental contact occurs, wash thoroughly with water.
- To treat around the face, spray a bit into the palm of one hand. Dip a finger and carefully apply to forehead, cheeks, tip of nose, and chin.
- To avoid having DEET drip into your eyes, don't apply it to your forehead if you're sweating. Instead, tie a DEET-treated bandana around your forehead.

- Treat all exposed and semi-exposed skin. Roll up pant legs and sleeves and treat areas that mosquitoes might reach. Ankles are especially vulnerable.
- Treat clothing and hat as well. This will prevent ticks from clinging to your clothing, and it will create an all-around odor that is effective at keeping mosquitoes away.
- DEET can dissolve some plastics and synthetic fabrics, including rayon and spandex. Test items in an inconspicuous place before applying DEET broadly.
- Don't treat the front of your headnet. You don't want to breath DEET that much.
- Avoid DEET in concentrations over 30 percent on young children. Don't use it at all for children under two years of age.
- After application, wash hands and avoid touching eyes, mouth, nostrils, etc.

Planning

Gear

Techniques

Hazards

Hiking

Camping with Kids

Avoid Bites and Stings

DEET is also effective at discouraging other biting and stinging insects and arachnids, including fleas, black flies, deer flies, horse flies, bees, wasps, midges, chiggers, and ticks.

ARACHNIDS

Ticks, chiggers, and scorpions are not insects but arachnids—relatives of spiders. Ticks are disease vectors; chigger bites can cause severe itching; and a scorpion sting can be extremely painful, but only rarely fatal.

Ticks and chiggers can be discouraged through the application of DEET, by wearing long pants and sleeves, and by tucking pants into boots or socks.

After passing through tick habitat (long grass or any moist undergrowth), take a few minutes to inspect your clothing and exposed skin. It usually takes a tick several minutes before it attaches itself to your skin, and you can generally brush or lift them off with your fingers during this time. Deer ticks—carriers of Lyme disease—are tiny, only about the size of a printed period (.) before they engorge themselves with blood. Wearing light-colored clothing helps make them more visible.

↗
Use straps or cord to keep ticks out of your trouser legs.

If a tick attaches itself, grasp it on the head with tweezers and pull steadily until it releases. Do not coat it with petroleum jelly, touch it with a hot match-head, or use any of the other old-wives' removal methods. They cause the tick to puke its guts into your skin and increase the risk of disease transmission.

Blacklegged ticks (scale enlarged)
↓

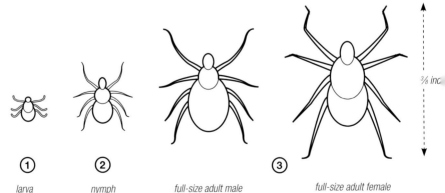

⅜ inc

① *larva*   ② *nymph*   *full-size adult male*   ③ *full-size adult female*

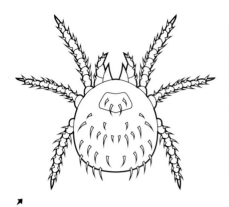

Chigger (actual size $^{1}\!/_{150}$ inch)

Chiggers, which are the larval form of a family of mites, live in almost any vegetation and are most numerous in early summer. They are so small as to be virtually invisible, but if you notice red welts or irritation, especially on your ankles, legs, groin, or waist, you've likely picked them up. Wash both skin and clothes in warm, soapy water to remove them, and apply an anti-itch treatment. Contrary to myth, they do not burrow beneath your skin.

Of 90 scorpion species in the U.S., all but four are found west of the Mississippi River, and only the bark scorpion, common in the Southwest, is dangerous. They are nocturnal, and shelter during the day under rocks and fallen wood, so be careful when lifting or turning over a potential hiding place. They are not deterred by insect repellent.

Scorpions occasionally crawl into hikers' boots if left outside a tent overnight. Shake out your boots and other clothes before putting them on. If you are stung, stop physical activity, apply a cold compress, and seek medical attention. If the sting is on an arm or leg, elevate it above the level of your heart.

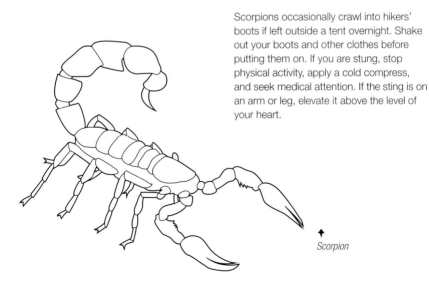

Scorpion

Planning

Gear

Techniques

Hazards

Hiking

Camping with Kids

Poisonous Plants

As long as you don't eat anything that you're not certain is safe, the only poisonous plants you need worry about are poison ivy, poison oak, and poison sumac. All three contain the allergen urushiol, which can cause an itchy rash through external contact. Poison sumac is by far the most virulent of the three, but all should be avoided.

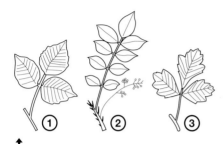

(1) Poison ivy, (2) poison sumac, (3) poison oak

TRANSMISSIONS AND SYMPTOMS

Urushiol is an oily substance on the surface of the leaves, stems, and other parts of poison oak, ivy, and sumac. It is a harsh allergen that causes dermatitis, and it remains present and active even if the plant is dead. Almost all people are allergic to urushiol, although some may not exhibit reactions after their first few run-ins. Don't get cocky. If you expose yourself often enough, you will become increasingly sensitive.

The oil is transferred to your skin by direct contact with leaves or other plant parts, or by secondary contact via clothing or by touching. Oil on your hands is transferred to everything you touch. If it is washed off promptly, the reaction will be minimal or none. The longer it remains on your skin, the worse it gets. Touching the eyes or mucous membranes can have serious consequences.

It usually takes from 12 hours to two days for a rash to appear, so it's important to recognize the plants and remove the oil as soon as you realize that you've contacted

them. Wash the skin immediately with soap and water. Wash or isolate shoes and clothes so that they cannot transfer the oil to skin or other items. Alcohol will also remove the oil, but if you use it on your skin, you will be more sensitive to subsequent contact with the plants for a while.

Once the oil is gone, the rash cannot spread to other parts of your body or to other people (although it may appear later due to a delayed reaction). As the rash progresses, blisters form and break open. The liquid that oozes from the blisters does not contain urushiol and can not spread the rash.

Prevention and Treatment

Barrier creams are available to keep urushiol off your skin. They are effective, but must be reapplied frequently, and it's still possible to transfer the poisonous oil from the surface of the barrier cream to unprotected parts of your body.

Itching may be treated with topical applications like calamine lotion and hydrocortisone cream, and with drugs such as antihistamines.

Not For Burning

Never burn poison ivy, oak or sumac in your campfire. The smoke contains urushiol, which can badly affect your eyes, sinuses and lungs.

Recognizing Poisonous Plants

Plant	Form	Leaves	Fruit	Range	Habitat
Poison Ivy	Groundcover or shrub	Green pointed leaves in groups of three. Tops shiny, bottoms dull. Red in fall.	Grayish-white berry-like drupes, present in the fall.	All U.S. states east of the Rocky Mountains, most Canadian provinces.	Below 5,000 feet elevation in most soil types. Partial shade, along edges of woods, stone walls.
Eastern Poison Oak	Shrub up to 3' tall	Green, lobed, resemble white oak. Orange or yellow in fall.	Small, round, yellow or greenish.	Southeastern U.S., from Virginia to Oklahoma and Texas.	Forests, thickets, open fields in dry sandy soil.
Western Poison Oak	Shrub, tree, or climbing vine	Usually 3 (up to 9) leaflets with scalloped, toothed, or lobed edges. Glossier than true oak. Bright green in spring, yellow-green or reddish in summer, red or pink in fall.	Greenish-white or tan berries.	Western coast of North America.	Oak and Douglas-fir forests, and on redwoods. Thrives in but does not need damp soil.
Poison Sumac	Shrub or tree up to 30' tall	7-13 leaflets, wavy-edged, oblong with a point. Green, turning red in fall. Bottom may be slightly hairy.	Round, flattened, less than ¼" across, in clusters	Primarily Deep South, but scattered throughout Northeast and Midwest.	Very wet or flooded soils, usually in swamps.

Planning

Gear

Techniques

Hazards

Hiking

Camping with Kids

Flood, Fire, and Falling Things

Although it's unlikely that you'll be threatened by a flood, forest fire, rockslide, or avalanche, it's important to know the nature of the risks and how to avoid them.

FLOODS

The most serious flooding typically occurs in—surprise!—flood plains, where a river cuts through wide-open, low-lying land. These floods are of little concern to campers, however, since they occur only after a lengthy period of heavy rainfall, when a river overflows its banks and spreads quickly over the surrounding flat land. In the unlikely event that you're still camping after several days of heavy rain, you'll have ample warning and should be long gone before the flood.

Flash floods, on the other hand, are a serious concern. These occur unpredictably in deep valleys or canyons below extensive mountains or other highlands. A heavy rainstorm over higher elevations can send large amounts of water rushing down many streams simultaneously: these collect and eventually meet miles away in a single valley or canyon, causing a wall of water to come rushing down what may be a shallow river or even a dry bed. Water levels can rise several feet in just seconds.

Fair weather is no assurance that you are safe from a flash flood, because the storm that creates it may occur miles away. Make it a rule never to camp immediately beside rivers in deep valleys or canyons. Signs of previous floods include areas of sand or bare rock beside the river where vegetation was swept away, and piles of deadwood and other debris that have collected above the current water level.

FOREST FIRES

In case of a forest fire, note which direction the wind is blowing. Is the smoke drifting toward or away from you? If you're upwind of the fire, travel into the wind to escape it. If you are downwind of a fast-moving fire, try to move around its flanks or cross natural fire-breaks like rivers or broad areas of sparse vegetation.

Fire climbs hills faster than it descends them, as the flames from burning vegetation light the vegetation above. Don't try to outpace a fire uphill. Instead, head down to the valley, where the ground and vegetation are likely moister and fire will spread more slowly.

Animals and birds fleeing in large numbers in one direction are a good sign of a fire that may be too distant to see, hear, or smell. Follow the land animals: they probably know the best path to safety.

Forest fires can be horrendously destructive, and causing one is possibly the worst thing that a camper can do. Should you lose control of your campfire, do absolutely everything you can to contain it, even if it means sacrificing your sleeping bag to smother the flames. You've nothing to lose by this, since you're certainly not going to take the time to pack the sleeping bag before fleeing.

ROCKSLIDES AND ROCK FALLS

Where rocks have fallen off a mountain before, they'll do it again. When hiking at the base of a mountain or cliff, observe exposed rocks present on the ground individually or in rows roughly parallel to the contours of the slope. When hiking in a steeply sloping valley between two hills, note whether the axis of the slope is strewn with rocks or has been cleared of vegetation or scored by falling rocks.

If you observe such danger signs, keep your ears open, and if you hear a falling rock, look for it right away. You can't outrun it, so run to one side of its path. Because the rock's course is unpredictable, move as far out of the way as you can.

Rockslides, mudslides, and landslides— where a large section of the side of a hill or mountain falls away all at once—cover areas of many square yards or even acres. Areas where these have already occurred are not normally dangerous except during and immediately following heavy rain, which may have loosened the soil holding the rest of the hill together. At such times, avoid adjacent areas both above and below the fall.

Should you dislodge a rock when hiking on hills or mountains so that it begins to roll downhill, immediately call out "Below!" or "Rock!" as loudly as you can to warn those below. This applies to any rock, regardless of size, for even a golfball-size stone can cause a serious head injury. If the warning comes from immediately above you, don't turn to face the danger: drop to the ground and cover your head with your arms.

AVALANCHES

Winter camping requires a high level of experience and special skills not covered in this book. Since novice campers generally restrict themselves to three-season camping, the chance that a reader will encounter avalanche conditions is relatively small, limited mostly to early spring in high elevations.

Most avalanches occur in predictable locations, and park rangers can usually warn you of areas to avoid. Should such information be unavailable, avoid snow-covered hills with slopes between 30 and 50 degrees, especially if trees are absent. Not only do trees and other vegetation tend to hold snow in place, but their absence may mean that they've been swept away by past avalanches. Be especially wary of a cornice— an overhanging shelf of snow at the top of a ridge. The risk of avalanche increases following rain and snowfall, and later in the day, when the sun has softened the snow.

Route your path around avalanche-prone areas, even if it means a significant detour. Only if this is impossible, cross the area early in the morning, when the air is cold and the snow is still solidly frozen. Don't worry about making noise as you travel: the notion that talking can trigger an avalanche is a myth.

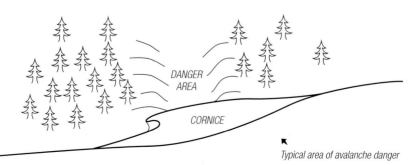

Typical area of avalanche danger

Planning
Gear
Techniques
Hazards
Hiking
Camping with Kids

Injuries and Illness

The vast majority of medical incidents that campers experience involve minor injuries that, while painful, are not likely to cause death or permanent bodily damage. Truly life-threatening medical emergencies are rare, but campers should be prepared to deal with both types of incidents. Although most first-aid responses are straightforward and easy to learn, a professionally-taught course in first aid will give you added skills and confidence.

First Aid

The first-aid descriptions in this chapter should be taken only as reminders or introductions to some of the more common camping injuries. Proper training from a certified first-aid specialist is advised, and all techniques should be practiced before being put to use in an emergency situation.

LEARN YOUR "ABC"

In any bad accident, such as a fall from a significant height or a bicycle crash, the first thing to do is ensure that the victim has the essentials for basic life functions. These are represented by the letters A-B-C, for airway, breathing, and circulation.

Airway

Make sure the airway is clear so that the victim can breath. Tilt the head backward, move the tongue out of the way with your fingers, and remove any foreign objects that may be lodged toward the back of the throat.

Breathing

Ensure that the victim is breathing by placing your cheek near his mouth to feel the breath, or watch carefully to see if the chest is rising and falling. If breathing is absent, perform rescue breathing. If you hear gurgling or bubbling, the victim may have inhaled vomit or water, or may have internal injuries causing the lungs to fill with blood. Position the victim on his side with his head downhill so liquids can drain out.

Circulation

Check for severe bleeding that could result in quick death, and ignore cuts that are "merely bad" at this time. Even catastrophic bleeding might not be obvious if the victim is wearing waterproof clothing, so check inside for pooling. If such bleeding is present, address it immediately. Next, check for heart function by checking the pulse. The pulse in the neck's carotid artery is the best, most reliable place to check. If there is none, begin cardiopulmonary resuscitation (CPR).

We all know never to move a person who may have a back injury, for fear of causing further nerve damage. This is good advice, but breathing and circulation must take precedence. If it is necessary to move the victim in order to ensure respiration and blood flow, do it, and risk the collateral injury.

RESCUE BREATHING AND CPR

Rescue breathing, a.k.a. artificial respiration, must be administered as soon as it's been determined that the victim is not breathing on his own.

1   Lay the victim on his back on a firm surface.

2   Tilt the head back and hold it there, pinching the nose closed with the same hand.

3   Use your other hand to open the victim's jaw and hold the tongue out of the way if necessary.

4   Inhale deeply, seal your mouth around the victim's, and exhale steadily for two seconds.

5 Lift or turn your head away and allow the victim's chest to deflate.

6 Repeat steps 4 and 5 every six seconds. Don't give up.

Check for a pulse. If it's absent, commence CPR. Traditional CPR consisted of alternating 15 chest compressions with two rescue breaths, but many experts now recommend "hands-only CPR," which is simpler and equally effective when performed by nonprofessionals.

1 Lay the victim on his back on a firm surface.

2 Open the front of any heavy coat or other thick or padded clothing.

3 Kneel beside the victim and place the heel of your open hand on the center of the victim's chest, over the breast bone (sternum).

4 Place your other hand on top of the first, with the fingers interlocked.

5 With your arms straight, press down hard on the chest at least 100 times per minute. The chest should depress 1½–2 inches.

6 Keep going until heartbeat and breathing resume or you are physically unable to continue.

The American Heart Association has a good hint for remembering and maintaining the rapid pace for chest compressions: it's the beat of the Bee Gees' song *Stayin' Alive*.

In all cases where the victim's life is at immediate risk, make every effort to contact medical professionals first of all. For example, if you're in an area with cellphone coverage, call 911 (or have someone else call) even before you begin CPR.

HYPOTHERMIA

Hypothermia occurs when the body's core temperature drops to 95°F or lower, and it is one of the most common causes of death in outdoor recreation. One reason for this unfortunate fact is that it can be difficult to distinguish from simply feeling cold, so its seriousness is often not recognized in time. Common factors leading to hypothermia include: cold temperatures, high wind chill factor, inadequate clothing, and wet skin or clothing.

Symptoms
- Shivering
- Slurred speech
- Very slow breathing
- Cold, pale skin
- Lack of coordination
- Fatigue, loss of energy
- Confusion, memory loss

Don't be misled by the cessation of shivering. If other symptoms persist, then the situation is becoming more acute, because the body's efforts to generate warmth by shivering have stopped.

Treatment
1 Move the victim out of the cold and protect him from wind.

2 Have the victim lie down. Use a sleeping pad to protect him from the cold ground.

3 Remove wet clothing, including socks and underwear. Dress him in warm, dry clothing.

4 Put him in a sleeping bag.

5 Heat water, put it in water bottles, wrap the bottles in towels, and apply them to the head, neck, chest, and groin. Be careful to avoid scalding the victim.

6 If the victim doesn't begin to warm up quickly, join him in the sleeping bag to provide extra warmth.

7   If the victim is fully conscious, let him drink a warm beverage like bouillon or herbal tea. Avoid beverages with caffeine or alcohol.

8   Watch for signs of shock and treat accordingly.

Don't rub or massage the victim or warm his limbs. The blood is coldest in the extremities, and you don't want to encourage circulation there that would send cold blood into the body's core.

These measures, if taken promptly, will suffice for mild cases, and the victim should recover fully in short order. For more serious cases, keep the victim warm and quiet and seek medical assistance.

HEAT EXHAUSTION

Heat exhaustion is caused by excessive loss of water and salt from the body. It can take hold rapidly as a result of heavy exercise, heavy perspiration, and inadequate fluid or salt intake, especially in hot, humid weather among people who are unaccustomed to hard exercise.

Symptoms
- Faintness or dizziness
- Fatigue
- Nausea
- Heavy sweating
- Rapid, weak heartbeat
- Skin cool and pale
- Low fever
- Cramps
- Headache
- Dark urine

Treatment
1   Move the victim to a shady, cool place.
2   Lay the victim on his back; elevate his feet and legs.
3   Loosen or remove the victim's clothing.
4   Have the victim drink cool water or sports beverage.

5   Cool the victim by fanning or by spraying or sponging with cool water.

6   Observe the victim for signs of heat stroke.

HEAT STROKE

Heat stroke is a far more dangerous—often deadly—condition that occurs when the body's internal temperature is too high. Its causes are similar to those of heat exhaustion.

Symptoms
- Body temperature greater than 104°F
- Headache, irritability, confusion, dizziness
- Fainting, coma
- Rapid heartbeat
- Rapid, shallow breathing
- Elevated or lowered blood pressure
- Lack of sweating
- Nausea

Treatment
1   Move the victim to a shady, cool place.
2   Seek medical assistance.
3   Remove the victim's clothes.
4   Have the victim drink cool water or sports beverage if able.
5   Cool the victim by fanning or by spraying or sponging with cool water.
6   Do not allow the victim to return to regular activities. Evacuate for medical observation.

SUNBURN

Sunburn symptoms usually appear within a few hours of excessive exposure to the sun's UV rays. It is easy to avoid by wearing UV-blocking clothing and applying sunblock ointment, but it's an all-too-common condition, especially among those who haven't spent much time outdoors recently.

Symptoms
- Burning pain
- Red skin
- Swelling
- Blistering
- Occasionally: headache, fever, fatigue

Treatment

1 Move out of direct sun.
2 Apply cool water. Take a bath or shower, or apply a cloth moistened with water.
3 Apply moisturizing skin lotion or aloe vera several times daily.
4 Do not lance blisters, but if they break, apply antibacterial ointment.
5 Take pain reliever such as aspirin, ibuprofen, or acetaminophen.

Do not apply butter, egg whites, petroleum jelly, or other home remedies.

SHOCK

Shock occurs when internal organs are not receiving sufficient oxygenated blood. Watch for it in combination with other injuries or serious medical conditions. Act promptly, as shock can result in permanent organ damage or death.

Symptoms

- Skin is cool, clammy, may be pale or gray.
- Fast, weak pulse. Low blood pressure.
- Breathing slow and shallow, or victim may hyperventilate.
- Nausea, vomiting, chills.
- Eyes appear dull, pupils dilated. Victim may stare blankly.
- Confusion or anxiety.

Treatment

1 Seek medical assistance.
2 Lay the victim on his back with feet about a foot higher than head. Loosen belt and tight clothing.
3 Check for pulse. If absent, administer CPR.
4 Keep the victim warm.
5 If the victim is not fully conscious, turn him on his side to keep airway clear.

Do not administer beverages, even if victim is thirsty.

ALTITUDE SICKNESS

Altitude sickness is the result of insufficient oxygen entering the bloodstream at high altitudes. It's common in sea-level dwellers who suddenly find themselves above 7,000 feet. The higher you go and the harder you work, the more common and acute it becomes.

Symptoms

- Confusion; mood changes; drunken behavior
- Lack of coordination; inability to walk a straight line
- Shortness of breath; dry coughing
- Dizziness, nausea, headache

Treatment

1 Rest for a day or two. Avoid strenuous physical activity.
2 Go to a lower altitude for the night.
3 Administer aspirin or acetaminophen for headache.
4 For serious cases, give supplemental oxygen or evacuate.

BURNS

Burns are a common camping accident, due mainly to unfamiliarity or carelessness with camping stoves and campfires.

Symptoms

- First-degree burns: skin is red and sensitive
- Second-degree burns: blisters form, swelling occurs
- Third-degree burns: skin is charred or burned away; underlying tissue may be charred or "cooked"

Treatment

For first-degree burns, see treatment for sunburn, above. For second- and third-degree burns, do not use burn creams, butter, or other applications. Instead:

1 Cool the injury with cold water for at least ten minutes.
2 Lay gauze or a sterile pad over the wound.

Planning

Gear

Techniques

Hazards

Hiking

Camping with Kids

3 Fasten dressing gently to undamaged skin well beyond the wound.

4 Administer aspirin or acetaminophen for pain.

SPRAINS

A sprain is a partial or complete tear to a ligament, one of the tough fibrous bands that connect bones together at a joint. Ankles and knees are the most commonly affected joints and the most debilitating for hikers.

Symptoms
- Pain
- Swelling
- Difficulty using the joint

Treatment
The treatment regime for sprains can be memorized by the acronym "RICE", which stands for Rest, Ice, Compression, Elevation:

Rest: Avoiding putting weight on the injured joint. You need not immobilize it, however. Gentle movement is advisable if it is not painful.

Ice: Apply a cold pack or immerse the joint in an icy bath as soon as possible after the injury. Apply ice for 15 to 20 minutes, four or more times daily for the first two days.

Compression: Wrap the joint with an elastic bandage.

Elevation: Raise and rest the joint above the level of your heart as often as possible.

FRACTURES AND DISLOCATIONS

A dislocation occurs when the bones of a joint are forced out of their normal alignment with each other. A fracture is a broken bone. Fractures may be "open," in which the broken end of a bone protrudes through the skin, or "closed," in which there is no penetration. Fractures vary in severity and the amount of displacement between the broken parts. First aid is similar for both types of injuries.

Symptoms
- Extreme pain, especially during movement
- Swelling
- Deformity of the limb or joint

Treatment
Do not attempt to set a broken bone or "reduce" a dislocation by forcing the bones back into proper alignment. Without X-rays and proper training, this could cause more serious injury. Instead:

1 Stop any bleeding in the case of an open fracture.

2 Immobilize the affected part with a splint and/or a sling. Keep breaks and joints at their present angle.

3 Evacuate the victim for medical treatment.

CUTS

So familiar that they require no description or list of symptoms, cuts and scrapes are the most common injury requiring first aid.

Treatment
For minor wounds, apply gentle pressure with a clean cloth for up to 30 minutes. More serious injuries may require greater pressure. Elevate the injured part if possible. If blood continues to flow after 30 minutes, reapply pressure and seek medical attention.

1 Clean the wound by flushing with clean water. Use tweezers to remove any remaining particles. Use soap only around, not in, the wound. Do not use disinfectants such as hydrogen peroxide or iodine.

2 Apply a double- or triple-antibiotic cream or ointment containing bacitracin, polymyxin B, and, optionally, neomycin.

3 Cover the wound with gauze and tape or an adhesive bandage to keep it clean and exclude harmful bacteria.

Survival Situations

In outdoors parlance, a survival situation involves being lost or being without water, food, or shelter. Of these, shelter is usually the most critical need, for one can die of exposure in a matter of hours, whereas one can survive for a couple of days, at least, without water, and two weeks or more without food.

LOST

Knowing where you are is among the most fundamental aspects of outdoors safety. Lose yourself, and you may soon be without adequate food, water, or shelter. Fail to show up when expected, and you may cause others extreme anxiety and set in motion a search-and-rescue effort. To the extent that this might really save your life, this is good. However, since it could have been avoided, it can also be viewed as a huge, unnecessary expense and a tremendous inconvenience to others. You owe it to others to stay found.

When you're in the wilderness, never leave your group without giving clear instructions about where you're going and when you will be back.

S.T.O.P.

Should you become lost, or even just unsure about your position, stop walking and run through the steps of the mnemonic "STOP," for Stop, Think, Observe, and Plan:

Stop, sit down, and calm down. Above all, do not go walking off in a direction that *seems* or *feels* right, hoping that it is right. The outdoor literature is full of examples of lost individuals who literally walked in circles following their sense of direction.

Think carefully about your most recent movements. What direction did you come from? What was your last known position?

Observe your surroundings. Do you see or have anything that will help you find your position or identify direction? A tree or rock that you noticed from a different vantage? A hill or stream that you can identify on your map? A compass? The position of the sun?

Plan your next move. If you can identify a landmark, how will you get there, and how will you proceed from that point? If you have no means of establishing location, your best option may be to sit tight and await rescue, so plan how you will do that safely and comfortably.

Partially Lost

Even without a map, a compass can help you get unlost, because instances where a camper has no clues at all regarding his location are relatively rare. If you know only your general bearing relative to a geographic feature, then you can find your exact location by traveling toward it. For example, if you know you're "somewhere south of Lost River," travel north until you either reach it, or can identify a hill, stream, or trail that appears along the way.

Leave Word With Others

Before leaving on a trip, leave a written description of your plans with a friend who will contact the proper authorities should you fail to return or report in on time. Include your planned location, route, timing, names of all participants, and contact information for the local authority your friend should contact.

Planning

Gear

Techniques

Hazards

Hiking

Camping with Kids

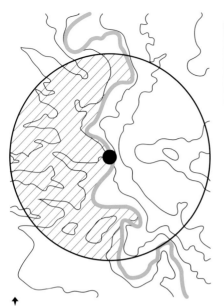

The dark spot beside the river (shown in green) is your last known position. If you know you're still east of the river, you can eliminate all areas to the west.

Find your last known position on the map. If you know how fast you walk and how long you've been walking, you can draw a circle around your last position that encloses the area where you could possibly be. You may be able to eliminate part of the circle from consideration: for example, it's on the wrong side of a river, or the terrain doesn't match what you've been walking through. Now that you've narrowed your location down, things should seem a lot safer and you'll probably be able to identify landmarks to pinpoint your position.

GETTING FOUND

Two kinds of situations might occur in which you need to call attention to yourself and make your location as visible as is possible: getting thoroughly lost, and being unable to travel due to an injury in your party or being stranded by a blizzard or other natural occurrence.

Finding North Without a Compass

Forget about moss growing on the north side of trees. It does. And on the south, east, and west sides too. The only reliable ways to identify direction without a compass are by reference to heavenly bodies. The following methods are all for the northern hemisphere:

Polaris, **the North Star:** Most people recognize the Big Dipper. Follow the line of the two stars at the end of the dipper's bowl upward, away from the bottom of the bowl. That line leads to *Polaris*, the star at the end of the handle of the Little Dipper. *Polaris* is almost directly over the North Pole.

The Sun: In the United States, the sun rises not from the east but from somewhere in the southeast, and it sets somewhere in the southwest. The exact direction of rising and falling varies with the season, but the path the sun takes across the sky is always approximately east–west. Push a stick into the ground and place a pebble at the end of the stick's shadow. Wait until the shadow moves a foot or so and place a second pebble at its new location. A straight line between the pebbles is roughly east–west. If you face the east–west line with west on your left, then north is in front of you. The closer to noon you do this, more accurate it will be.

The Sun and a Watch: At noon, the sun is due south. At any other time, hold an analog watch parallel to the ground and point the hour hand in the direction of the sun. South is halfway between 12 and the hour hand. If you have a digital watch, draw a clock face showing the current time on a piece of paper and orient it as above. These instructions apply to Standard Time. Adjust accordingly during Daylight Savings Time.

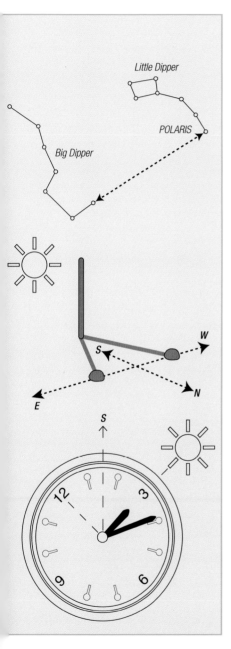

Naturally, no one will come looking for you unless they know you're missing, hence the importance of leaving written plans with a friend, including instructions of who to contact, and when, if you're overdue. Many wilderness areas have check-in points where you sign in and out. Make use of these, for rangers check them to see who's in the area and who's left.

If you have reason to believe that you'll be searched for, there's much you can do to improve your chances of rescue:

Sit tight: The more you move around, the harder you are to find. If you are depending on rescue, stay in one place.

Be visible: Make camp in a place that's visible from the air and from the surrounding land. If you must shelter under trees for weather protection, advertise your presence in a nearby open space.

Prominent location: If possible, place your camp on a prominent natural feature such as a lake shore or an exposed ridge. Air-search pilots look for these features to help themselves navigate.

Increase contrast: Spread out materials that provide visual contrast with the background: for example, bright fabrics on dark rocks or dark clothing on white sand.

Flags: Make flags out of clothing or tarps. In any wind, the fluttering motion will attract searchers' attention.

Ground signals: Lay patterns of rocks or sticks on the ground, or tromp patterns into snow or sand. It's not necessary to spell out S.O.S.; a big X will draw a searcher's attention. The bigger, the better.

Planning

Gear

Techniques

Hazards

Hiking

Camping with Kids

Active Signaling

Making your camp visible is a passive measure. You can also actively draw attention to your presence if you see or hear searchers.

Light a fire: Allow it to burn brightly at night. In daylight, dark smoke is much more visible, so pile live vegetation on the fire and allow it to smolder. It is generally not practical to keep a fire burning nonstop, so prepare it so that it can be lit quickly on the first indication of a search team's proximity, like the sound of a distant aircraft.

Reflected light: If searchers appear between you and the sun, you can use a mirror or other reflective surface to flash light in their direction.

Noise: A whistle is far more effective if you want to be heard than shouting.

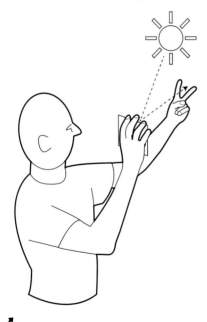

↗
Frame your target between two fingers like a gun sight, and aim the mirror so that it reflects the light against those fingers.

SHELTER

Your primary shelter is the clothes you wear. In a survival situation, take care to keep your clothing dry, clean, and intact. (Yes, cleanliness counts! Most fabrics insulate better when clean.) If you lack adequate insulation even after donning two or more layers, stuff the space between them with dry leaves or pine needles.

If you lack a tent, you should build a shelter. In addition to providing weather protection, a shelter makes your location more visible, and it's a big psychological aid to have a "home" when all else seems lost. The type of shelter you build will depend upon the materials available in your given location.

Squirrel Nest

This is really just a pile of leaves, but it can keep one person surprisingly warm and even moderately dry. Gather a huge pile of leaves, then excavate a trough in the middle. Lie down in the trough and pull the leaves over you. There should be two or more feet of leaves on top of you. If possible, make your pile between two fallen logs four or five feet apart: this will help keep the leaves in place.

Turn left   *This is the trail*   *Turn right*

↗
If you must travel while expecting to be searched for, use trail marks to indicate your direction.

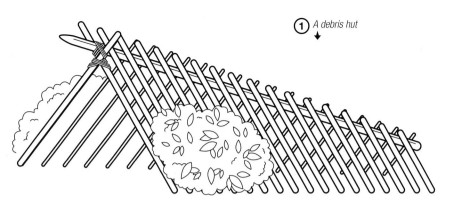

① *A debris hut*
↓

1. Debris Hut

A debris hut requires a good knife and some strong cordage. You can make it big enough to sleep two.

Tie two sturdy sticks together in an X, with the top legs very short. Stick the longer ends in the ground and make sure you can crawl under it with several inches to spare. Place one end of a strong straight branch at least 10 feet long on top of the X, and lay the other end on the ground. Collect 30 or 40 sticks and lean them against both sides of the long ridge pole.

Make a huge mound of leaves over the side-sticks. Place more sticks or branches over the pile to hold the leaves in place. Stuff more leaves inside the hut, and pile a few big arms-full right by the "door." After you wriggle into the hut feet-first, pull the pile in after you to help keep heat in.

2. Shade Shelter

Desert campers must protect themselves from sun and heat during the afternoon, the hottest part of the day. A shade shelter can be built with a knife, a little string, and just a few long sticks and some vegetation.

Make a tripod from three long poles. If it's breezy, dig the bases of the poles a few inches into the ground. Tie a few shorter

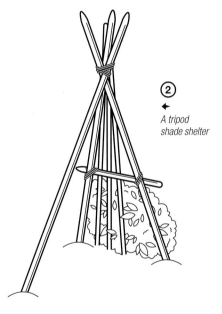

②
←
A tripod shade shelter

sticks horizontally between two adjacent poles. Pile sagebrush or other available vegetation against them, tying it in place if necessary. One can also use clothing in place of vegetation.

A second side of the tripod may be covered for additional protection against a night breeze. You can even enclose the third side to capture warmth, as long as you leave enough space to enter and exit.

Planning

Gear

Techniques

Hazards

Hiking

Camping with Kids

3. Tarp Shelters

Should your tent be lost or damaged, a very adequate shelter can be improvised with a tarp, or even a sheet of polyethylene. A simple rectangular tarp can be set up in numerous configurations, approximating a tent with or without a floor, a lean-to, or a cross between the two.

The trick to setting up a tarp that doesn't sag or flap excessively is to pitch it over a ridge pole or a tight rope that serves as a ridge. If your tarp lacks grommets, tie each corner tightly around a small stone, and tie off the tarp from the stone.

Two trees at an adequate distance are often the easiest anchor for a tarp shelter.

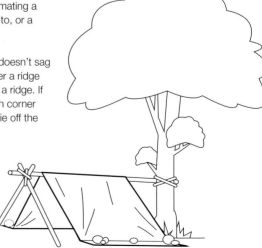

➜

Lashed, crossed sticks can support one or both ends of a ridge pole.

4. Quinzhee

Unexpected heavy snow can make walking impossible and an emergency shelter essential. Luckily, the snow itself provides all the material you need to build a *quinzhee*, a kind of DIY snow cave that is far easier to build than an igloo.

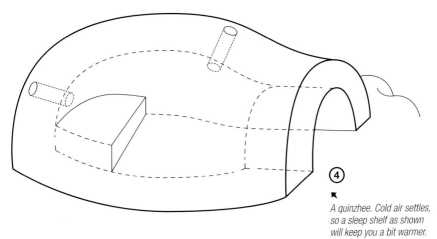

A quinzhee. Cold air settles, so a sleep shelf as shown will keep you a bit warmer.

For a two-person quinzhee, make a pile of snow at least 10 feet long, 6 feet wide, and 6 feet high. If the snow is light and powdery, pile it higher and wait at least 30 minutes for it to settle. Cut a bunch of thin, foot-long sticks and push them into the mound all around so that their ends are flush with the surface. Start digging like a dog at one end of the pile, shoveling the snow out between your legs. When you can fit inside, start expanding the space upward and outward. Stop when you expose the ends of the sticks. You should have enough room to lie down at full length and to sit or kneel. To avoid the buildup of carbon dioxide, make two fist-size air passages on opposite sides of the mound. One should be nearly vertical and the other horizontal. Check them frequently to make sure they remain clear.

FOOD

Outdoor literature suggests that individuals who have not previously practiced hunting or trapping skills will have a very poor rate of success in a survival situation. Furthermore, carbohydrates are far more important than proteins for abating your hunger and satisfying your near-term nutritional needs. If you have fishing gear, by all means use it, but count on plant food to keep you going.

Most areas have an abundance of wild plants to keep you reasonably well-fed during most seasons of the year. Learn about common forage foods in your region before heading into the wilderness. The next page runs through a few of the more common ones favored by survival experts.

Planning

Gear

Techniques

Hazards

Hiking

Camping with Kids

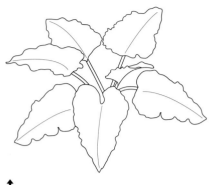

↑
Burdock

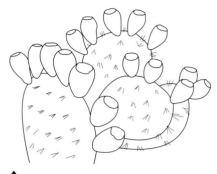

↑
Prickly pear

Burdock root: Burdock is an artichoke relative found all over North America except in the Deep South. The inedible leaves are 2 feet long, 1 foot wide, and white and fuzzy on the bottom. The flower, which looks like a thistle, grows on a stalk up to 9 feet tall. The main edible part is the large taproot, which can be harvested from early spring through late fall by pulling it out of the ground. Scrub off the dirt, slice it thin, and simmer or sauté until soft.

Cattail: Found in dense stands in shallow water and very wet ground throughout the United States, cattails grow up to 12 feet tall and have an easily recognized seed head that looks like a big frankfurter. Young shoots can be peeled and cooked or eaten raw. The hearts are good sautéed.

Prickly pear: Common in the Southwest, this cactus is easily recognized by its flat green pads. Reddish-purple fruits appear from the middle of summer to late fall. Wear gloves when cutting pads from the plant. Cut out the spines. Peel the pad, or burn it to remove the stinging hairs. Roast the pads whole, or slice and steam them. The fruit can be eaten raw, but spit out the seeds, which cause gas pains if swallowed.

Thistle: Many species are distributed widely throughout the United States. Musk thistle (*Carduus nutans*), spear thistle (*C. vulgare*), marsh thistle (*C. palustre*), cabbage thistle (*C. oleraceum*), wooly thistle (*C. eriophorum*), and cotton thistle (*Onopordum acanthium*) all have edible stems and stalks. Wearing leather gloves, start cutting away the uppermost spiny leaves and branches, and work your way down. Next, remove the spines from the stem by scraping up and down with your knife. Cut the stem off near the ground, then peel off the tough outer fibers. Young stems can be eaten raw; boil older, tougher ones.

FIRE

See pages 100–102 to review basic fire-building skills. In a survival situation, the additional essential skill is the ability to light the fire without matches or a lighter.

Lighting a Fire with Sparks

Flint and steel is the best-known method of creating sparks with which to light a fire. The steel should be of the high-carbon variety, not stainless. (The blades of outdoor knives may be either.) The "flint" need not be true flint: other hard minerals, including agate, chert, jasper, and quartz work too.

Build a teepee-style fire lay with kindling, and place tinder inside, leaving a golfball-size space in the middle. Make a ball of the finest, driest tinder, press a depression in the middle, and place it on a dry leaf. Hold the steel firmly over the tinder ball and strike it with an edge of the flint at about a 30–degree angle. It's the carbon in the steel that makes the sparks, and the objective is to shoot the sparks onto the tinder. If your steel is a knife blade, strike against the spine, not the edge, to protect the blade and your striking hand.

As soon as you have live sparks on the tinder, blow on them gently until the tinder takes fire. Lift the leaf and place the burning tinder inside the teepee, then build up the fire in the usual manner.

Fire Plow

Anyone who ever tried to make fire by simply "rubbing two sticks together" knows it's not as easy as it sounds. The trick is to rub the sticks fast enough to generate a dense little pile of wood dust that's hot enough from the friction to set fire to tinder.

A bow drill is the most effective way to do this, but it takes quite a lot of work to fashion the three main components. A fire plow is simpler to assemble and nearly as efficient.

The base can be any piece of dry, sound (i.e., not rotten) softwood reasonably flat on one surface and 2-3 feet long. The plow is a hardwood stick at least an inch in diameter. Chisel-point one end of the plow with your knife, and blunt the opposite end to protect your hand. Place a green leaf partly under one end of the base, and hold the other end down with your foot or knee, or sit and rest it on your thigh.

Press the plow against the base at a 30–45-degree angle and push it forward. After several strokes, you will begin to wear a bit of a trough in the base. Keep "plowing" the trough, pressing down hard and stroking rapidly so that hot bits of wood dust begin to collect on the leaf. It's essential to work quickly and without pausing. When enough hot dust has collected into a little mound on the leaf, transfer it into your waiting tinder pile and blow gently until it takes flame.

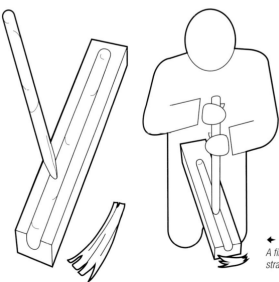

← *A fire plow is simple to make and straightforward, but not easy, to use.*

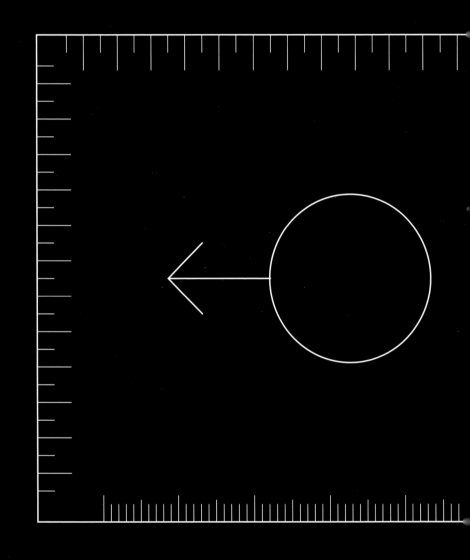

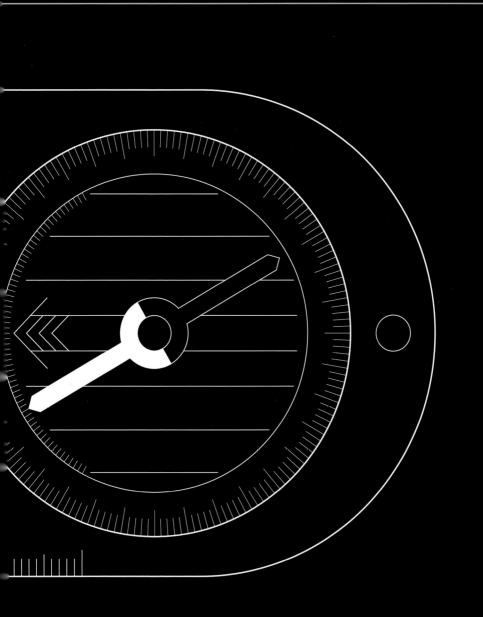

Planning

Gear

Techniques

Hazards

Hiking

Camping with Kids

A Hiking Day

A day of hiking consists of a series of events: the start, rest breaks, lunch, possibly a rugged climb, a peak summit with a great view, a stop to collect drinking water or take a swim. Approaching these events systematically—knowing what to expect and when—will give you a series of goals to achieve. This will help keep fatigue at bay and make the day more fulfilling.

MORNING

Getting started in the morning is full of ambivalence. On one hand, mornings are often chilly and it's nice to stay in a warm sleeping bag. On the other, we like to click off a good chunk of mileage before the heat of the afternoon slows us down. As soon as dawn breaks, one member of the party usually emerges from the tent to get things moving. Once the stove is lit and the water is boiling, it's a hard heart and an iron bladder that can remain in the sleeping bag much longer.

Coordinate efforts so that one person washes up the breakfast things while another takes down the tent and so on, so that everyone is ready to roll at about the same time. Review your plan for the day, referring to the map and trail guide and taking note of challenging climbs, water sources, and other important features. Then hit the trail, but expect to stop a few times during the first half hour while people adjust their loads, retie their boots, and generally get into the rhythm of walking.

ON THE TRAIL

Plan to take a 10-minute break every hour to rest, drink water, and grab a handful of gorp. If the weather is cold, make sure that extra clothing is readily accessible to prevent rapid cooling of warm muscles.

For most backpackers, lunch is a simple, quick affair, involving no cooking except perhaps to boil water for instant soup or tea. After a half hour, it's back on the trail again, alternating hiking with brief rests until the day's destination is reached.

DAY'S END

Many like to end their day's hiking mid-afternoon, and spend the rest of the daylight relaxing, reading, sketching, and preparing for supper and the night. In very hot weather, some hikers will find a patch of shade, take a nap or bathe in a stream during the worst of the afternoon heat, and then continue hiking until dusk.

If light begins to fade before you reach your intended campsite, look around for a *bivouac*—an *ad hoc* campsite. Hiking in the dark can be dangerous, and it's easy to lose the trail. Better an uncomfortable sleep than a sprained ankle or getting lost.

Gradual Energy Release

Eat both sugary and high-carbohydrate foods for trail snacks. Candy and energy gels will give you a quick burst of energy, while gorp and granola bars release their calories more gradually.

Distance

Whether you're planning a day hike or a month-long trek, it's essential to know the distance you'll cover and to estimate your rate of travel. From that information, you can calculate the amount of time required and how much food, water, and fuel you'll need.

DISTANCE AND DURATION

Trip planning can be approached from two directions: by the trip, or by the day. Say you've heard of a nice loop hike (one that takes you back to your starting point without retracing your steps) that starts at a parking area on Old County Road, climbs to the top of Mount Prospect, descends the other side of the mountain, wends through Pinegrove Woods, and ends back at the trailhead. Your trail guide says the loop totals 18 miles. If you know how long it will take you to cover that much ground, then you can determine how many nights you'll be out and how much food to pack.

On the other hand, let's say you have a three-day weekend to go camping. Subtract a half-day to drive to the trailhead: that leaves two and a half days for walking. If, from experience, you know you can comfortably cover 10 miles per day under average conditions, you should plan a trip no longer than 25 miles (2.5 days X 10 miles). Then dip into your guidebook or ask a local outfitter to recommend a hike of that length.

Mileage on the Map

Guidebooks list distances for defined trips on specific trails, but you may want to plan your own hike. You lay out your large-scale topographic map and string several trails together to take you up and down a mountain you've been wanting to climb and next to a lake that's reputed to have awesome fishing.

Use a measuring wheel to measure the length of the route on the map. (If you don't have a measuring wheel, bend a piece of thin wire to follow every turn on the trail, then straighten it out and measure its length.) Then convert the distance on the map to distance on the ground. For example, if the route measures 16⅞ inches on the map, and the scale is 1:24,000:

16.875 inches x 24,000
= 405,000 inches = 6.39 miles

HOW FAST?

Only experience will tell you how fast you travel, but if you're planning your first backpacking trip, you have to start with a reasonable estimate.

The average adult walking speed is about 3 miles per hour, but that assumes easy conditions quite unlike those you will face. You will be carrying a pack, going up and down hills, walking on uneven surfaces and possibly tricky terrain, and stopping to navigate, rest, and sightsee. Most experienced hikers average about 2 miles per hour on average terrain. If you're a newcomer to backpacking or out of shape, your speed will be lower.

Significant climbs also slow things down. A rule of thumb calls for an additional hour for every 1,000 feet of *vertical gain* (see definition on page 147). Of course this will vary with your fitness, experience, and the nature of the climb. A rise of 1,000 feet on a well-maintained footpath will obviously go faster than 1,000 feet on a hill covered with *scree* (loose rocks).

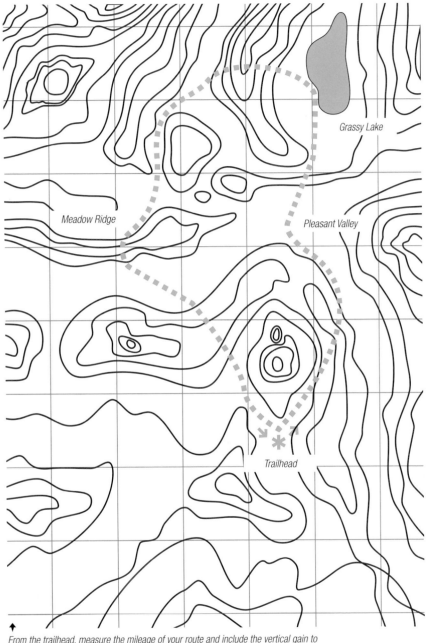

Grassy Lake

Meadow Ridge

Pleasant Valley

Trailhead

From the trailhead, measure the mileage of your route and include the vertical gain to estimate how long you'll need. See text for example.

Planning

Gear

Techniques

Hazards

Hiking

Camping with Kids

Vertical Gain

Vertical gain is the total amount of uphill climbing on a trail, with no adjustment for downhill travel. If you climb up and down a 600-foot hill, your vertical gain is 600 feet, even though you end up with no net change in elevation.

Factors Affecting Speed and Distance

- Fitness
- Experience
- Elevation
- Elevation gain
- Grade (steepness)
- Trail surface/conditions
- Weather
- Hours of daylight
- Weight of pack
- Number in party (larger groups move slower)
- Speed of the slowest member of the party

Let's revisit the trip in the previous section. If that 6.39-mile route involves elevation gains totaling 740 feet:

Distance: 6.39 miles ÷ 2 miles per hour = 3.2 hours (i.e., 192 minutes)

Climbing: 740 ft. x 1 hour/1,000 ft. = 0.74 hours (i.e., 45 minutes)

Total time: 192 minutes + 45 minutes = 237 minutes (i.e., 4 hours)

For trips lasting more than a day, note the location of campsites and water sources, and make sure you'll be able to reach these important points within your daily schedule. Write your daily plan in a journal, noting where you'll camp, where you'll collect water, possibly a nice prospect where you'd like to have lunch, and any planned side-trips or downtime for fishing, rock-climbing, or other activities. Mark the route on your map with a highlighter pen to make it easier to follow in the field.

Be careful not to overestimate your endurance when starting out. Most beginning backpackers find 6 to 8 miles plenty to cover in a day. As you build experience and endurance, you might easily double that figure. Some hikers might even triple it. But on your first few trips, be conservative lest you find yourself behind schedule and too sore or exhausted to move.

Slow and Steady Sets the Pace

The slowest walker sets the pace for the party. No one likes to hold up the group, and faster walkers must accept that slower ones are moving at their best pace consistent with safety and endurance. Fast walkers must therefore learn patience, for it is unfair and unwise to try to force a slow walker to go faster. For their part, slow walkers must resist pressure to move at a pace beyond their judgment.

Never leave the slowest member of the party behind to "catch up." Although some experienced backpackers hike alone, this is inadvisable generally, and especially so for beginners. Groups of four or more can split into smaller groups according to speed. Agree where the groups will meet, and distribute gear so that the faster group can prepare lunch or begin setting up camp before the slower group arrives.

Hiking Skills

Is there really anything to learn about *just walking*? Well, yes. Although you've been walking all your life, you probably haven't been doing it over rocks, up and down mountains, and through streams with 30 pounds of gear on your back. There are indeed special techniques for hiking safely and efficiently.

PACE AND POSTURE

When you start out at the beginning of a day of hiking, you're fresh and full of energy and the inclination is to set a rapid pace. Resist it, for it will tire you quickly. Set a pace you can keep up all day, even if it seems slow at the start. The end result will be more miles covered and less fatigue.

Hold your torso tall and straight and, where the path is clear, keep your head up and your eyes ahead—not only to see what's coming, but to enjoy the view. Only where the footing is less secure do you need to watch the placement of every step. Unless you're using trekking poles, keep your hands empty and free: don't stuff them in your pockets or hook them behind your pack's shoulder straps.

HILLS

When climbing hills, place each step flat on the ground and resist the inclination to come down onto and take off from the front third of your foot, the ball and toes. On really steep ground, conserve energy with the "rest step," which momentarily takes the weight off of your leg muscles and transfers it to your leg and hip bones:

- Take a step forward with your right foot, but keep the weight on your left.
- Straighten the left knee and push it back slightly to lock it.
- After a slight pause, shift your weight to your right leg and use it to lift your body up and forward until your right leg straightens. Lock the right knee briefly.
- Repeat until you reach the top of the hill.

↑
Steps to the rest step

Descending hills can be hard on ankles, knees, and hips. An extra 30 pounds on your back places your joints under an unusual amount of stress, and this is compounded if every downward step lands with a jolt. Proceed slowly downhill, keeping your knees bent and taking small steps. If your feet slide forward inside your boots so that your toes get jammed in front, stop and tighten the laces in front of the instep. Failure to do so may result in blistered and bruised toes.

Trekking poles have a lot going for them. They increase a walker's stability by providing an extra point of contact with the ground. They transfer some of the effort of walking to the arm muscles, and they absorb some of the shock that would normally affect the leg and hip joints. With some specialized tents, they can serve as tent poles, so the net additional weight they represent may be close to nil.

To hold trekking poles properly, insert your hands through the straps from below, then bring your hand down to grasp the strap and

Planning

Gear

Techniques

Hazards

Hiking

Camping with Kids

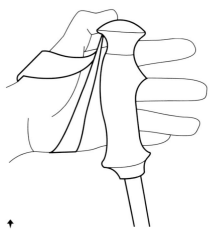

↑
Gripping a trekking pole

the grip together. Set the length so that they reach the ground in front of you when your elbows are held at a 90-degree angle. Swing them as you walk in a natural movement, setting the point on the ground an instant before the opposite foot.

When climbing a hill, push down on the pole to help lift your weight. When descending, lengthen the poles so that you can put weight on them in front of you without bending forward.

↗
Gaiters

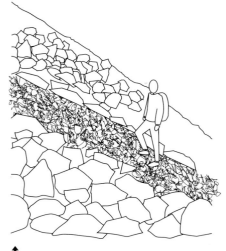

↑
Scree slope

SCREE

On slopes above the treeline, it's common to encounter scree—large fields of loose, small stones that tend to slide downhill as you step on them. Walking either up or down scree slopes is difficult, so route around them if possible. But if you must walk on scree:

- Ascend scree slopes in a series of shallow zigzags, keeping your feet sideways to the slope.
- If you must ascend straight up, splay your feet outward and take short, quick steps.
- Do not run or slide downhill. Use the zigzag pattern to descend, or take sideways steps, keeping your feet perpendicular to the slope.
- Larger rocks amidst smaller scree tend to be more stable. Step just above them (not on them) as good solid anchors for resting or for a good forward thrust.
- Avoid walking directly below another hiker on scree.
- Gaiters are useful to keep small stones out of your boots.

Planning

Gear

Techniques

Hazards

Hiking

Camping with Kids

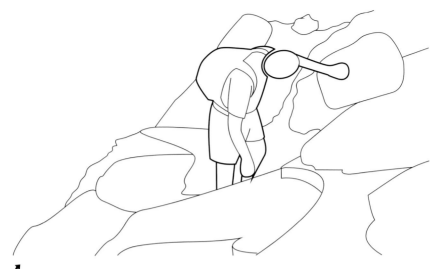

↗
Rock scrambling

ROCKS

Some hiking trails require a bit of rock climbing, but rarely of the sort that requires special equipment or technical skills. (*Never* do that sort of climbing without proper training!) To safely climb rocks:

- Place heavy items as low in the pack as possible. Because weight should be packed higher for general trail hiking, this may mean repacking before you climb.
- Strap trekking poles to your pack. Keep your hands empty for balance and climbing.
- Tighten the pack's shoulder and hip straps to prevent it from shifting.
- Test all handholds and footholds before committing your entire weight to their safety.
- Keep your body as close to the rock face as possible.
- Of your four points of contact (two hands, two feet), make sure that three are stable and secure before moving the fourth to a new position.

- Keep as much of your boot sole in contact with the rock as possible. Don't climb with your toes.
- Use your leg muscles to lift your weight, and your arms primarily for stability.
- When descending, face the rock and look under your armpit for footholds. Do not go down in a seated position, facing away from the rock. You cannot grab a handhold that's behind you.
- If you get nervous or scared, find a stable position (sitting, if possible), then pause. Give yourself time to calm down before carefully considering your next move.
- Don't take chances, exceed your confidence limits, or urge others to do so.

Most hikers find climbing up rocks easier and less worrisome than climbing down them, because it's easier to see foot- and handholds above you than below. For this reason, avoid climbing up rocks near the limits of your ability and confidence if you'll have to come down them later. But be assured: if you climbed up it, you *can* climb down it safely.

STREAMS AND RIVERS

Many hiking trails cross streams and small rivers. Most of the time, this is an inconvenience at worst, but it can be dangerous in some situations.

Crossing by hopping from one boulder to another is risky unless you can test each one before committing your weight to it. Be extra careful of rocks that are wet or covered with algae or moss. Wade if you can't cross safely dry-shod: it is far better to get wet intentionally than to risk falling onto rocks or into the water.

If you wade:

- Avoid wading rivers more than waist-deep. In the case of whitewater, don't go over knee-deep.
- Rivers are shallower where they are wider (unless a new tributary adds more water to the flow). Be prepared to travel upstream or downstream along the bank until you find suitably shallow water.
- Beware of starting a ford from the inside of a bend in the river. The outside of bends tend to be deeper.

- Wear foot protection. Change into sports sandals or sneakers if you have them and keep your hiking boots dry. If you must wear your boots, be extra careful when you resume hiking to avoid the blisters that wet boots often cause.
- Unbuckle your pack's hip belt and loosen the shoulder straps. If you fall, you want to be able to get out of your pack quickly.
- Use trekking poles or a walking stick to provide a third or fourth point of contact with the stream bed.
- Feel your way with your feet. Maximize contact with the bottom by shuffling your feet.
- Face upstream and travel diagonally upstream or downstream, not straight across.
- Cross together by locking arms at the elbows. Place stronger walkers in front and behind.
- Beware of catching your foot between two rocks. Even in shallow whitewater, a fall with an entrapped foot can be deadly, because the current will make it difficult to stand back up.

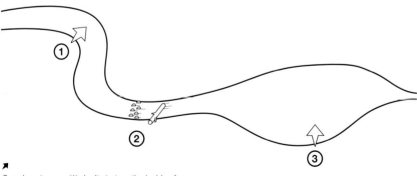

Crossing streams: (1) don't start on the inside of a bend as it will be deeper near the opposite shore; (2) use stepping stones or fallen trees only if you can step carefully and test each one; (3) wider sections of a stream are often shallower.

Planning

Gear

Techniques

Hazards

Hiking

Camping with Kids

Foot Care

The success of your hiking trip depends on the health of your feet. Allow a blister to form and then go untreated, and you will—at best—have a miserable time. So if that's the best, what's the worst that could happen? How about: being unable to walk; having to be evacuated; suffering from a serious infection. Are those bad enough for you?

BLISTER AVOIDANCE

Never begin a backpacking trip with new boots. New boots must first be broken in under less demanding conditions. (See page 53.) If your foot shifts around inside your boot, a blister is almost certain to result. Tie the laces tighter, wear thicker socks, or get a better-fitting pair of boots.

The most common areas for blisters are the toes and the bottom and back of the heels. If you are prone to blisters in these or any other location, protect them before you put on your socks in the morning. Most hikers rely on synthetic moleskin, which you can cut with scissors to the appropriate size and shape. One side sticks to your skin, while the other slides smoothly against your sock or boot to reduce friction. Some hikers cut a round hole in the moleskin to fit over a particularly sensitive area, then cover that piece with a second piece of moleskin without a hole. Other options include adhesive bandages, first-aid tape, and duct tape.

Wear well-padded hiking socks or clean, thin inner socks made of a sweat-wicking fabric with thick outer socks. Keep them dry, and change them if they get wet. Pack at least two pairs of the liner socks so that you can wash one pair every night and wear the other the next day. On the trail, remove your boots and socks occasionally during your ten-minute snack breaks to inspect your feet, air them out, maybe wash them, and shake out any debris, down to the smallest grain of sand, that has collected in your boots and socks.

BLISTER RESPONSE

Blisters can form after just a few seconds of irritation, so the moment you feel something rubbing or irritating your foot, stop and take care of it. Remove your boot and socks, inspect the sensitive area for redness, and apply moleskin. Figure out what is causing the irritation and remove or fix it. A creased sock, of course, can be smoothed out, and debris can be removed. If it's the boot itself—perhaps an internal seam of stitching that's rubbing—cover the offending feature with moleskin or duct tape, or wear another layer of socks.

If a blister has already formed, you'll have to puncture and drain it. The only alternative—allowing it to break without your careful intervention—is worse, and it certainly will break if you continue hiking. So clean your hands and the area around the blister thoroughly, then sterilize a needle in a flame (a match will suffice). Allow it to cool, then puncture the blister near the bottom edge. Press the blister from the top, forcing out the fluid. Dry it, then apply a dab of antiseptic cream followed by a sterile dressing and moleskin.

If a blister has already formed and broken, disinfect the wound before dressing it, and vow to pay closer attention to the signals your feet send you in the future.

Navigation

Many hiking trails in popular areas are well marked, requiring little in the way of navigation and only that you pay attention. Other trails may be marked poorly or not at all. As you gain experience, you will likely want to leave the more popular paths and strike out in new directions. But even if you stick to marked trails, navigation skills can help you identify your location along the trail, the geographic features you see, shortcuts or emergency exit routes, or your location should you lose the trail.

Eyes Open

Even well-marked trails can be confusing sometimes, especially where they are joined by unmarked footpaths or animal trails. Learn to keep your eyes up and observe not just the walking surface, but your surroundings. Take note of distinctive trees, rocks, and other features that you will remember and recognize, even if you approach them from the opposite direction. At every intersection of paths or other places where you have to make a directional decision, stop and observe: take careful note of the direction from which you came. Never leave sight of the trail, even for a sanitary break, without performing this recognizance.

READING A TOPO

The topographic map is the most important navigational tool, and in many cases it will satisfy your navigation needs without a compass. While topos show roads, streams, lakes, buildings, and some trails, their most important feature is contour lines.

Each contour line connects a continuous series of points at the exact same elevation. If you were to follow the path of a contour line, you would go neither up nor down, but you might walk a very curvy route. The distance between the lines on the map, and the shape of the lines, can tell you a great deal about the landscape.

The vertical distance represented by adjacent contour lines varies with different maps, ranging from less than 10 feet to more than 100 feet. This contour interval is always indicated. Every fifth contour line is a little darker to make it easier to count intervals.

Where contour lines are close together, it means a large change in elevation over a short horizontal difference—in other words, a steep slope or a cliff. The closer the lines, the steeper the slope. Some other important land features (illustrated on the following page) that can be identified by contour lines include:

Individual hills, mountains, and peaks: These appear as roughly concentric circles, ovals, or other closed curves.

Saddles: Concentric barbell-shaped closed curves indicate two nearby hills or mountains connected by a stretch of ground higher than the surrounding land.

Ridges: A series of parallel Vs, usually along the side of a hill or mountain. The narrow end of the V points downhill.

Valleys: Also a series of parallel Vs, but between two hills or mountains. Where a river flows through a valley, the narrow end of the V points upstream.

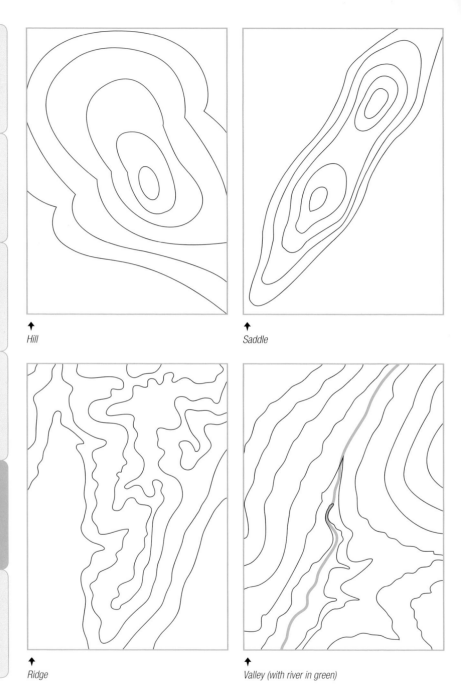

Planning

Gear

Techniques

Hazards

Hiking

Camping with Kids

↑
Hill

↑
Saddle

↑
Ridge

↑
Valley (with river in green)

Inaccuracies in Topo Maps

Topo maps may contain inaccuracies. Lakes and swamps may appear or vanish due to human or natural processes; streams may change their course or dry up; new roads and trails may be established and old ones abandoned and allowed to grow over. Check the map for its latest revision date, and trust it accordingly.

USING A COMPASS

A compass has three main uses:

Map to field: To determine the direction to a certain geographic feature in the field from your present (known) location on the map.

Field to map: To find your location by comparing the direction of features in the field with features on your map.

Maintaining a course or bearing: To travel in the right direction toward a destination you can't see.

The following instructions assume the use of a baseplate or orienteering compass. These are the most popular type among backpackers, because they are easy to use, lightweight, and inexpensive.

✦

Compass parts: (1) baseplate, (2) direction of travel arrow, (3) magnifier, (4) scales, (5) index pointer, (6) orienting lines, (7) orienting arrow or gate, (8) needle

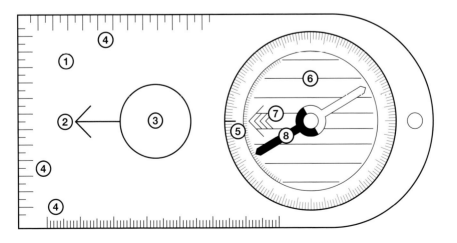

Planning

Gear

Techniques

Hazards

Hiking

Camping with Kids

True, Magnetic, and Declination

The Earth has two north and two south poles. The geographic or true north and south poles represent the axis of the Earth's rotation. (The north–south lines of longitude that appear on all maps, including topos, are aligned with true north and south.) The *magnetic* north and south poles are where the compass needle points, drawn by the Earth's magnetic field.

In the northern hemisphere, the two poles are separated by about 500 miles—close enough for navigation, as long as we correct for the difference. (The location of the magnetic pole wanders a bit from year to year, but not enough for us to worry about.)

The difference between the geographic and magnetic poles is measured in degrees of *declination*. Declination varies depending on your location. From the East Coast of the United States, magnetic north is to the west of true north, and the declination, measured in degrees between them, varies with your exact location. On the West Coast, declination is east.

For some compass procedures, we need to make adjustments for declination. All topo maps indicate the amount of declination east or west in degrees, so the adjustments are simply a matter of adding or subtracting.

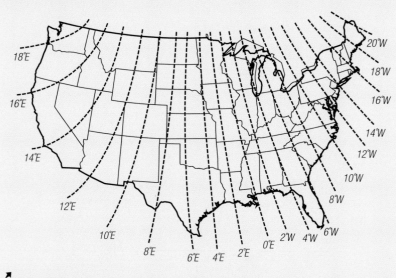

↗

Declination between true and magnetic north changes with your location.

➜

This symbol on a USGS topo map indicates true north (★), magnetic north (MN), and grid north (GN), which is often the same as true.

MAP TO FIELD

Situation

You know your location on the map and your destination. You either can't see the destination from your current location, or you think you might lose sight of it while hiking due to intervening trees, hills, or fog. There are no trails between the two, so you will have to bushwhack (travel cross-country). You need to know the direction to travel.

Procedure

Using a straightedge, draw a pencil line between your starting and ending points on the map. If the line doesn't cross a line of longitude (one of the vertical lines of the map grid or the edge of the map), extend the pencil line so that it does, or draw a parallel line that does.

1 Place a long edge of the compass baseplate on the pencil line with the direction-of-travel arrow pointing in the direction you will travel and the compass dial over a line of longitude.

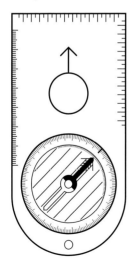

Magnetic course direction

Once you know the magnetic course to your destination, just follow the direction-of-travel arrow while keeping the magnetic needle in the "gate."

2 Holding the baseplate motionless on the map, turn the dial so that orienting lines are aligned with the map's north–south grid lines and the north arrow on the dial points north on the map. (Ignore the magnetic needle for now.) The index line now shows your true (not magnetic) direction of travel on the dial's degree scale, but you're not going to use that information here.

3 Holding the compass firmly against the map, turn them both together until the north end of the magnetic needle (usually red) is inside the red "gate" (or "shed") indicating north on the dial. The direction-of-travel arrow is now pointing directly at your destination in the field.

4 Lift the compass from the map without changing its direction or turning the dial on the baseplate. Hold it level in front of you, a little above belly-high, with the direction-of-travel arrow pointing straight ahead.

5 Start walking in the direction indicated by the direction-of-travel arrow while keeping the magnetic needle in the gate (i.e., pointing north on the dial).

6 Every time the needle shifts out of the gate, you need to adjust your direction to bring it back in. As long as you do that and keep the direction-of-travel arrow pointing straight ahead, you'll be heading toward your destination.

Trust Your Compass

The more you trust your sense of direction, the more it can mislead you. A gut feeling that you're heading the right way is no substitute for a compass bearing.

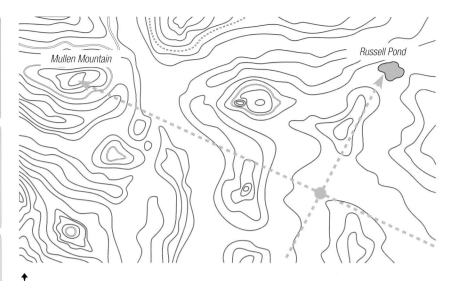

Planning

Gear

Techniques

Hazards

Hiking

Camping with Kids

Mullen Mountain

Russell Pond

↟

If it's 294 degrees to the peak of Mullen Mountain and 29 degrees to the end of Russell Pond, there's only one place you can be (circled).

FIELD TO MAP

Situation

You have only a rough idea of your position. You can identify some features in the field but need to know where that places you on the map.

Procedure

Choose two landmarks that you can see in the field and identify on the map (e.g., mountain peaks, a bend in a river, a fire tower or other structure). They should be at least 20 degrees apart, but wider is better. The exact angle isn't important.

1. Aim the compass's direction-of-travel arrow at one of the landmarks.
2. Holding the baseplate stationary, turn the dial so that north aligns with the north end of the magnetic needle (i.e., place the needle in the gate).
3. Still holding the baseplate stationary, turn the dial again to adjust for declination. For example, if declination is 18 degrees east, turn the dial counterclockwise so

that the magnetic needle aligns with 18 degrees. If declination is 10 degrees west, turn it clockwise so that the needle aligns with 350 degrees on the dial.

4. Place one of the front corners of the baseplate on the landmark on the map, then pivot the entire compass around that corner until the orienting lines are aligned with the grid and the gate is facing north. Draw a pencil line along the edge of the baseplate that runs through the landmark. Extend the line with a straightedge if necessary. You are somewhere along this line.

5. Repeat steps 1–4 for the other landmark. Your location is where the two lines cross.

6. For greater accuracy, take a bearing to a third landmark. If the three lines don't cross at exactly the same point, your location is within the triangle they form.

MAINTAINING A COURSE IN THE FIELD

You may be able to see one mountaintop from atop the adjacent mountain. The crow can fly it in a straight line, but once you descend into the valley between them, you will probably lose sight of both your starting point and your destination. Constantly referring to a compass can be awkward and slow, but it is possible to maintain a straight course toward an unseen destination without a compass.

From your starting point, identify at least two objects that are directly in line with your direction of travel. These objects might be trees, rocks, or distant mountain peaks. Walk toward them, and as you near the first object, identify a third object, further distant than and in line with the second. Keep sighting along two or more objects in a line, replacing each with a new target as you pass it. Look back periodically to confirm that the guideposts that you passed are still in the same line. If at any time the more distant object is set to disappear before you reach the nearer one—for example, a distant mountain may be obscured below the horizon of a closer stand of trees—pick a different, closer object for your second guidepost.

Useful Navigation Instruments

If you can estimate your speed, a watch will give you a good idea where you are on a trail or other known course. Use your watch's stopwatch function, or jot down the time when you pass known positions in a notebook or directly on your map.

An altimeter is another useful navigational tool when used in conjunction with a topo map. If you stick to a trail, your elevation will show you where you are along the side of a mountain.

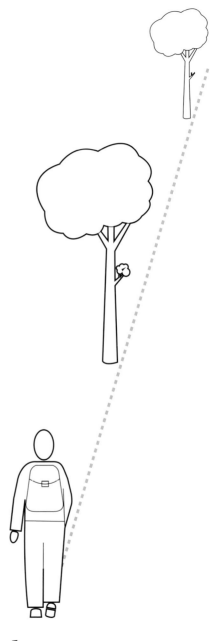

↗
Maintaining a straight course

DETOURS

Except in flat open country, it's rarely possible or practical to maintain a perfectly straight path for any long distance. Swamps, cliffs, thickets, private property, fences, and all other manner of obstacles are likely to get in the way, but there are several strategies to get around these while maintaining your overall course and not losing track of your position:

1. Contour detour: Rather than climbing up and down steep hills along a straight path, you may be able to follow a contour line. Of course lines of elevation aren't drawn on the earth, but by walking around the side of a hill or mountain and climbing neither up nor down, you'll eventually end up on the opposite side. The distance may be greater than a straight line, but the walking may be easier.

2. Intentional error: Even if you do a good job maintaining your course, you're unlikely to hit some targets dead-on. If your destination is small and hard to see—like a campsite in the woods—you might pass within 50 feet of it on either side and not know it. But if the campsite is along a feature that you can't miss, like a trail or a stream, you can simplify the job of finding it. Since you can't aim at it directly with 100 percent confidence, aim intentionally 5 or 10 degrees to one side of it. Then when you reach the stream or the trail, you'll know which direction to turn. It increases the distance of your walk a little bit, but it beats guessing the wrong direction

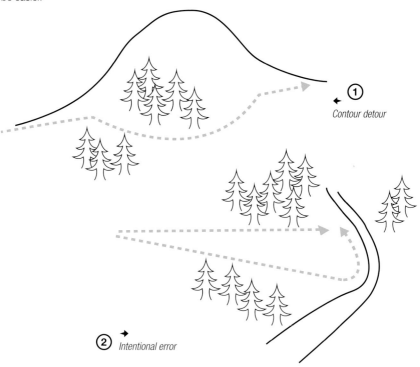

① Contour detour

② Intentional error

Planning

Gear

Techniques

Hazards

Hiking

Camping with Kids

3. Right-angle detour: When you encounter the obstacle, check your map to see whether an easier path exists to the right or left of your course. Turn the dial on your compass 90 degrees so that the direction-of-travel arrow points toward your new temporary course. Keeping the magnetic needle in the gate, walk far enough in that direction to get around the front of the obstacle, then turn the dial back to your original bearing. Walk along that bearing until you have passed the side of the obstacle, then turn the dial 90 degrees in the opposite direction to bring you back to your original line of travel. To make sure your two side-trips are the same length, use a stopwatch if progress is regular and predictable, or else count paces.

4. Follow the feature: Following any linear feature that appears on the map, such as a stream, trail, road, stone wall or fence, is often an easier way to travel and stay aware of your position than following a compass course.

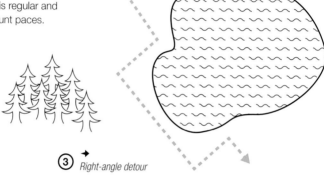

③ *Right-angle detour*

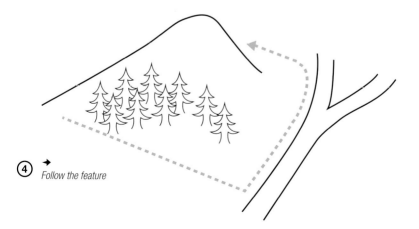

④ *Follow the feature*

6 CAMPING WITH KIDS

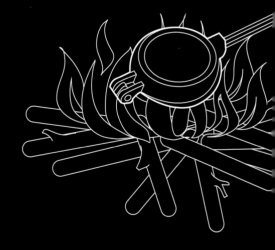

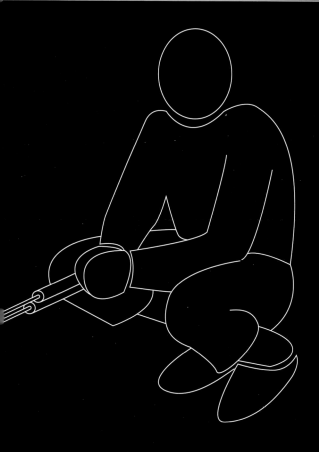

Attitude and Teamwork

Planning

Gear

Techniques

Hazards

Hiking

Camping with Kids

Attitude, as they say, is everything. If you introduce your child early to the outdoors, when you as a parent are still both fully in charge and hugely respected, the child will quickly come to love it. If you wait until the child is older, has developed strong preferences and habits, and no longer believes you're the smartest individual who has ever strode the Earth, then instilling that love for camping might prove more challenging, but with some creative parenting, you'll find it's still worth the effort.

AGE AND CAPABILITY

Infants' needs are pretty straightforward and easy to satisfy. Car-campers and RVers can easily pack enough gear to keep an infant fed, warm, dry, and clean. Canoeists can too, but they should stick to waters that are so thoroughly calm and protected that there is no chance whatsoever of a capsize. Backpacking trips of a night or two in duration are possible if one adult carries the infant in a front carrier or sling and a second adult carries all the gear. Bicyclists should pursue other styles of camping for a year or so because there's no good way to carry an infant on a bicycle.

Toddlerhood brings new capabilities to the child and different challenges to the adult. A child can ride on a bicycle child carrier or in a bike trailer when his neck muscles are strong enough to support the weight of his head and a helmet against a certain amount of jarring. Usually after the child's first birthday, therefore, short bike-camping trips become possible, with one adult hauling the child and another carrying most of the gear. Around the same time, a child can make the shift from a front-pack to a backpack-style child carrier. Backpacking trips must still be short, however, because the adult carrying the child can't haul gear as well.

Oddly, things can become more difficult as a child's walking becomes more proficient. By the age of two or three, the child is too heavy and impatient to carry any distance in a backpack carrier, but not capable of walking very far on his own, and certainly not able to carry his own gear. Children of this age may get antsy riding in the center of a canoe or in a bicycle child seat or trailer. Automotive camping seems to be the best option, but even then, the child's ability to walk means a greater capacity for getting into trouble, so parents must remain unusually vigilant.

↗
Child carrier

Some time around the age of 5 to 7 years, children become more capable of following instructions, respecting limits, and walking farther. They can carry a small amount of gear in their own packs, wield a canoe paddle, and pedal a tag-along or co-pilot-type bike trailer—none of these very long or effectively, it must be said, but they are now beginning to take an active role in the camping endeavor. As before, trips should be short, and breaks must be frequent to maintain the child's energy and interest. Children of this age can also begin to help with camp chores.

By the age of 10, a child can walk or ride as far as many adults. They can carry much, but perhaps not all, of their own backpacking gear. They can lend a useful hand with a canoe paddle and may be mature enough to deal with the consequences of a capsize in not-too-serious conditions. They can maintain a reasonable pace on their own bicycle, but shouldn't carry more than a token amount of bike cargo yet. And they can, and willingly will, take on full responsibility for many camp chores—more, perhaps, then you make them do at home.

From there on, a child's competence, strength, and endurance only increase. It's your responsibility as a parent to nurture the interest you've begun to instil, to continue their outdoors education, and to look after their safety with an ever-lengthening tether.

GET THEM INVOLVED

The key to gaining and maintaining a child's interest in camping is to get them involved in the process early and keep them involved throughout the trip.

Plan Together

Approach the trip planning process in a true spirit of cooperation: some of it is for the child, some of it is for the adult, and hopefully, everyone will enjoy most of it. Examine maps and guides together and find destinations, activities, and sights that are a mix of what the child and the adult want to do. Remember that a child's range of experience is limited; he may not understand what some of your suggestions entail and will not know whether he will enjoy them until he's actually exposed to them.

This applies to menus and gear lists too. If the child sees that his favorite meals are included, he'll likely be accepting of yours. (If not, don't worry. Camping makes people hungry. If the child has no recourse to other options, he really will eat what you make.) Lay out clothing, sleeping bags, and other gear along with the luggage it all has to fit in, and discuss what's needed, what's wanted, and what just won't fit.

Kids Plus One

Tweens and teens who do not relish the idea of spending a lot of time with their parents might be talked into a camping trip if allowed to bring a friend. Friends will keep each other occupied and may provide a buffer to Bad Attitude Syndrome.

Planning

Gear

Techniques

Hazards

Hiking

Camping with Kids

Tasks and Responsibilities

Show the child how certain gear works, and talk about the chores or other responsibilities he will have. Your everyday experience to the contrary, most kids crave responsibility if it's real and substantial and they understand the point.

Some young children worry about sleeping arrangements and wonder what it will be like sleeping elsewhere than their familiar bedroom. If this is the case with yours, set up the tent together in your back yard, lay out the sleeping pads and bags, and spend some time together in it. You might even spend a night there before leaving on your "real" camping trip. Some children may enjoy taking full responsibility for setting up the tent. Younger ones can assist by holding the stakes and handing them to you when you need them, and collecting them when it's time to break camp.

Here are some other chores that children of various ages might perform:

- collecting firewood and tinder
- collecting and filtering water
- lighting the camp stove
- cooking
- cleaning up after meals
- policing the campsite before leaving
- caring for younger children
- navigation
- keeping a trip journal or maintaining a photographic record of the trip

You'll notice that the above list covers virtually all camping chores except chopping wood. Of course not all children are capable of handling all of these responsibilities in all their aspects. Much depends upon the child and the specific nature of the task. For example, a child who might reliably navigate along a well-marked trail can't necessarily be trusted to maintain a course while bushwhacking through unfamiliar terrain. You'll have to make these judgment calls carefully with your own child's capabilities

in mind. If you can't yet trust him to do it alone, perhaps you can share responsibility by involving him in the process.

I'm a strong believer in giving children true responsibility early. You might not agree with this approach, but I've found it successful. Yes, it's true, that lighting a camping stove is a potentially dangerous task, and no sane parent would just toss their child the lighter and say "Here. Figure it out." But a good teacher will:

- explain the procedure and its potential dangers
- demonstrate the procedure
- talk the child through the procedure while monitoring it carefully
- after several successful monitored trials, turn the responsibility over to the child with strong confidence and satisfaction that the child has just gained a skill and taken a step toward maturity

Limits

The other side of the coin is limits: what tools they may not use or touch, where they may not go. Discuss these too while still at home, and issue reminders when arriving at every new campsite.

Some limits are easier to impose than others. "Never touch the axe" is suitably absolute and easy to follow. "Never leave the campsite," is trickier, because there are no fences or white lines indicating exactly where the campsite ends, and it's often tempting to go just a couple paces farther to examine a curious fungus or follow an interesting butterfly. When you see the child two steps off the campsite and you don't object, then two more steps really doesn't seem like an infraction after all.

No-Shoe Rule

Two rules worth enforcing strictly (for both children and adults) are: no shoes in the tent, and no food in the tent. Both are important to keeping sleeping bags clean. The no-food rule also helps keep critters away.

Real responsibilities make children part of the team

In Camp with Kids

Most kids prefer to spend time in camp rather than on the trail, the river, or the road. Limit travel to just a few hours a day. Once they're in camp, kids have a fantastic capacity for keeping themselves amused.

KEEP IT INTERESTING

For a child to enjoy camping, the experience must be diverse, and it must include activities of particular interest to the young mind. Few children have the patience (never mind the physical endurance) for hours of trail hiking. Think of how less interesting it would be to ride behind someone on a bike or in a backpack carrier for hours on end. Some children will happily play with toys in the bottom of a canoe while you paddle across a lake, but even that gets old after an hour or so. Every kid wants to get up and run.

In most drive-in-style campgrounds, kids range freely (often on bicycles) and generally look out for one another. Relax. It may be the only time and place all year when you can set the kids free and not worry about them.

Younger children who must stay put can remain happily occupied for hours just playing with nature. A magnifying glass or nature scope (a combination magnifier and telescope) is all it takes to turn a bug into an hour-long observation project. Kids love to

Fun Camp Activities

No one activity is appropriate for all ages, abilities, camping styles, and locations. Use your judgment and your imagination. Bring the necessary gear along for some of the following activities, but also allow your child time for completely unstructured play of his own devising.

Physical Activities
- bicycling
- swimming
- ball sports (soccer, softball, etc.)
- flying disc games
- playground games (jump rope, hopscotch, etc.)
- canoe games and skills

Nature
- nature observation, identification, collecting (birds, insects, leaves, minerals, etc.)
- animal track identification and plaster-casting
- astronomy

- tactile materials play (sand castles, mud pies, water play)
- fairy houses

Camping Skills
- land navigation: map and compass games
- fire building
- cooking

Quiet Activities
- card games, board games
- reading
- puzzle books
- graphic arts (coloring, drawing, painting, print-making, etc.)
- fiber arts (sewing, knitting, etc.)

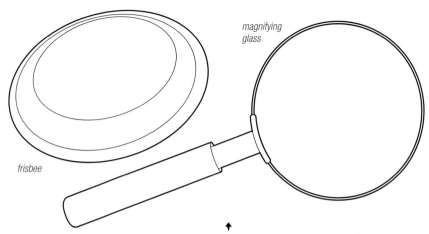

magnifying glass

frisbee

Keep the kids busy with toys and activities that
are easy to take with you on the trail.

play with water: set Junior beside a small
brook with a cookpot and a trowel, and he'll
spend all afternoon exploring hydrodynamics
and making dams and mud pies.

Tents make excellent playpens, as long as
they don't get too warm inside. Bring along a
few amusements for quiet activities like a
deck of cards, crayons, or a favorite book.
These will be especially valued if rain keeps
you inside for a day.

Bedtime
Some children will be so tired from a full day
of outdoor activities that they crash before
supper. Others may be too excited by the
experience to sleep, and a few might be
scared by the unaccustomed noises of the
woods or by the notion of dangerous night-
walking creatures, real or imaginary.

There's probably no good reason to impose a
standard bedtime rule in camp. If the child is
scared or excited, why not let him stay up
with the adults until he is ready for sleep? But
you can make bed a bit more enticing by
bringing along a child's plush toy and a glow-
stick or flashlight to play with or read by.
(Bring extra batteries.) Bedtime stories, of
course, are good. Avoid scary stories around
the campfire until the child is mature enough
to enjoy the fright.

It's all too easy for a sleepy, disoriented
child to lose his way en route to find the toilet.
Until he's fully comfortable about it, be ready
to accompany him if he needs to go in the
middle of the night. Another problem is what
to do if you need to go. Most children sleep
hard and will not wake if you duck out for a
couple of minutes. But waking up alone in a
strange place could be terrifying, so you
might discuss this with them beforehand.
Children who are old enough can be
instructed to count to 500, and that
you'll be back before they're done.

Planning

Gear

Techniques

Hazards

Hiking

Camping with Kids

Hiking with Kids

Kids need to work their way gradually into hiking. Start with hikes of less than an hour, and increase the distance gradually. After the child has built up the necessary strength and endurance, have him carry a daypack with just a few essentials: a small water bottle, a snack, and a windbreaker or sweater. While you could certainly carry these for him, most children crave the responsibility of carrying their own gear, and it's an urge worth nurturing.

EQUIPMENT

For the early forays, sneakers work just fine. Only after the child begins to carry a real backpack is the additional support of hiking boots needed.

When the time comes to graduate from dayhiking to overnight backpacking, don't just stuff more gear into the school backpack. Purchase a child-size backpack designed for camping, with proper suspension and other adult features like a hip belt and hydration compatibility. Build up the load gradually over the years, to a maximum of one-quarter of the child's weight. The child might start by carrying his own clothing, water, a snack, toilet kit, survival kit, and perhaps an item of personal interest like a nature scope. But Mom or Dad will have to carry his sleeping bag, pad, and other gear for a while longer.

Children should be clothed in the same layering system that works for adults: a wicking underlayer, an insulating middle layer, and a weatherproof shell. Although children do not sweat as much as adults, the extra insulation of the underlayer is still worthwhile to guard against hypothermia. Remember to pack a fleece cap too.

SET GOALS

The mere act of walking isn't very appealing to most kids. To keep them motivated on the trail, they need something to look forward to. A "glorious view" might not excite them, but summiting "the highest peak in the whole county" might be something they'd strive for.

Let them know how long it will take and offer encouragement. "It's two hours of hiking, but then we'll get to go swimming" (or fishing, rock climbing, etc.) is the way to do it.

PLAN ACTIVITY BREAKS

Schedule frequent activity breaks when traveling. These aren't the brief water-and-snack breaks that adult backpackers take every hour; they're *fun* breaks. If a swimming hole or rock wall isn't along your path, plan or invent activities. Here are some ideas:

- Practice map and compass use. Set up a small navigation problem with a reward at the end, like a favorite candy bar.
- Collect or identify bugs, leaves, minerals, animal tracks, etc.
- Have a squirt gun fight. (Keep them hidden in your pack as a surprise.)
- Make a fairy house.

Teach nature in small bites. Kids don't want an extended lesson in entomology, but if you point out one interesting fact about one interesting insect, it'll likely stick. Let the child determine some of the breaks and activities. If something catches his interest along the trail, indulge it.

One-Off Treat

For regular trail breaks, the child's favorite candy bar makes a nice change from the usual gorp or granola bars, especially if it's a surprise.

Safety

If you're new to camping, the potential dangers may seem imposing, especially for your children. A good piece of advice is to respectfully calm down and back off. While there are real hazards to beware of, the chances of anything worse than a trivial injury occurring are slim and easily minimized through common prudence. Camping is among the healthiest activities your child can participate in.

PROACTIVE, NOT OVERPROTECTIVE

Children tend to ignore physical discomforts—especially potential ones—until it's too late. Their skin burns more easily than adults', so apply sunblock frequently. Don't wait for them to tell you the mosquitoes are biting: be proactive with the bug dope. Until the child learns to recognize and avoid poisonous plants, apply a barrier cream to their skin and wash any clothing that might be contaminated with urushiol before it can spread.

On the other side of the coin, don't attempt to protect your child from every conceivable harm. Have you ever burned yourself on a stove, cut yourself with a knife, or tripped and fallen? Probably so. Just as probably, it left no lasting injury. Your child can't learn how to cook, use a knife, or run on uneven ground unless he's given the opportunity to make mistakes.

That said, certain hazards do bear special attention, such as:

Fire: You need only bring a toddler's hand close enough to a fire to feel the heat to impress upon him its danger. The real danger lies in carelessness. Children should never be allowed to run near the fire or play with burning sticks. Remind them that even after a fire has visibly died out, the fire ring and metal grate may remain hot.

Stoves: Keep children away from camping stoves until they're old enough to trust with matches and have some experience cooking at home. Probably the greatest danger is a scalding burn from a spilled pot, due to the unstable nature of many backpacking stoves.

Knives: Children as young as 5 or 6 can be taught to handle a knife safely and to use it effectively to point sticks for cooking hot dogs or toasting marshmallows. A lockback design is a good choice for a child's first knife.

Axes: Good arm, hand, and upper body strength, as well as good judgment, are needed to control an axe. Many children may be introduced to this tool at around age 11 or 12. Until then, it's strictly hands-off.

↗
Lockback knife

Planning

Gear

Techniques

Hazards

Hiking

Camping with Kids

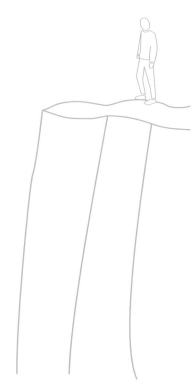

↗
Most kids don't spontaneously fall down from high places.

High places: Barring truly unusual wind gusts, no one ever falls forward when they're standing on the edge of a drop. But more than once, I've seen parents come close to pushing a child over the edge because they can't control a "protective" urge to grab them. (The child shies away when the parent tries to interfere, because the child understands the potential danger.) Be wary of allowing a child climb rocks, but trust him not to fall down for no good reason.

Foot injuries: Bare feet invariably suffer cuts, stubs, splinters, burns, or stings when camping. Prohibit going barefoot around camp and on the trail.

GETTING LOST

Up to a certain age, children should never leave the campsite unattended. The first measured step to independence is to allow them to move off the campsite as long as they keep it in sight. This is a useful rule when allowing young children to collect firewood.

No one—adults included—should ever leave sight of a campsite or trail without having the means to navigate back to it. The moment you wander into the forest without a compass bearing, the potential for getting lost becomes very real. It takes only a detour around a tree or two to lose your sense of direction.

Search and rescue professionals have the following advice for children and parents in a lost-child situation:

For Kids

- **Hug a tree:** The moment a child thinks he's lost, he should hug a tree (or a rock if he's not in woods). Staying in one place vastly increases the chances of being found quickly, and having a sizable physical object as a grounding point is comforting. The child no longer feels entirely lost, because he knows he's near his tree.
- **Safety gear:** Children should always carry a whistle and a plastic trash bag. A whistle can be heard much farther than a shout, and it requires less effort. The trash bag provides an emergency shelter. The child can either poke a hole in the bottom and wear it like a cape, or climb into it and bunch the open edges around his neck. (Pocket-size rain ponchos are a good alternative.)
- **Reassurance:** Some children have actively avoided rescuers because they were ashamed of being lost or fearful of being punished. Assure the child that, should he be lost, there will be no punishment, and you will be proud of his ability to get himself found.

- **Visibility:** Show the child how to increase his visibility to searchers by spreading out clothing, and creating ground marks with sticks or rocks. Explain that a person lying down and making snow-angel-like motions is more visible from the air than one standing up.
- **Animals:** Explain that animals do not want to eat children. If the child hears something at night, he should blow his whistle. If it's an animal, it'll be scared off. If it's a person, he'll be rescued.
- **More reassurance:** Remind the child that searchers will be looking for him; that their only concern is for his safety, and that staying in one place makes him easier to find.

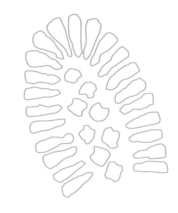

For Parents
- **Rules:** Make it a rule that the child may not leave the trail or the campsite without supervision.
- **Footprints:** Set a piece of aluminum foil on a towel and have the child step on it with both feet, wearing the shoes he will wear on the trail and in camp. Give the prints to searchers, who can use them to distinguish the missing child's tracks from other footprints.
- **Call for help:** Search areas increase exponentially with time, so call for help as soon as you realize the child is missing. Quick action will maximize the hours of daylight for searching and minimize the effects of exposure. Don't worry about issuing a false alarm: search crews would rather learn that the child is safe than search under desperate conditions.
- **Be available:** Once search crews are active, stay put and make yourself available to answer questions. This can be more productive than searching on your own.

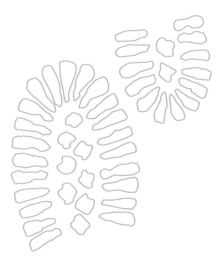

Take your child's shoe prints on aluminum foil.

Camp Cooking with Kids

Planning

Gear

Techniques

Hazards

Hiking

Camping with Kids

Many children get their first experience cooking when camping. This is a shame, since camp-cooking, while not difficult, is at least a little more difficult than cooking at home with the convenience of refrigerators, countertops, easily manipulated stoves, and hot and cold running water. Whatever the reason, if camp-cooking in general tends toward the uncomplicated, camp-cooking for kids who haven't cooked before should be stone-simple and fun.

SIMPLE COOKERY

Kids enjoy cooking food on a stick. Perhaps it's because it's an acceptable way to "play" with fire, or maybe it's because it's more hands-on and active than waiting for something to cook in a pot. Aside from the obvious safety issues, which can be easily taught, there are a few tricks to doing it right:

- Use a green stick that won't burn through quickly. It must be be stout enough to support the weight of the food without sagging unduly.
- The stick must be long enough to get the food over the fire without endangering or discomforting the user. For foods that take more than five minutes to cook, it should be long enough to prop with a stone outside the fire ring.

- Many foods don't adhere properly to cooking sticks: when you turn the stick, the food flops around so that the same side is always facing down. A stick with a forked end solves this problem.
- Never allow the stick to point down: you risk dropping the food.

Foil-wrapping is another cooking method that kids enjoy, probably due to its simplicity and its novelty (and maybe because it minimizes clean-up chores). While some foil-wrapped cooking can be done on a grill, cooking in coals adds to the fun because you're covering the food with something that looks a lot like dirt.

Foil wrap baking

Use heavy-duty aluminum foil or two layers of standard-weight foil with the shiny side facing in. Smear on a bit of butter or oil, then place the food in the middle of the sheet. Bring two opposite edges together, then roll the seam closed. Make several folds on both ends to seal the package. Place the food over hot coals, not in live fire, and use a stick to pile more coals on top. Be patient and allow enough time for the food to cook, because it's difficult to check for doneness without tearing the foil. Be careful of escaping steam when opening the package after cooking.

Cooking with pie irons combines the active involvement of stick-cooking with a totally novel cooking implement that is used only over campfires. Coat the outside of pie-iron sandwiches liberally with butter or margarine. Turn the irons every minute or two, and check the food frequently for doneness or signs of burning.

Kids also like foods cooked shish-kebab-style on skewers, probably because it's fun to eat food on a stick.

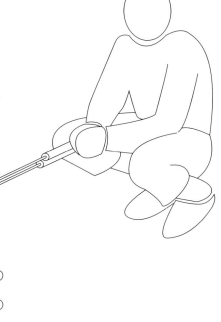

↗
Cooking with a pie iron

Chicken-Vega-Foil

Ingredients
- cooking oil
- 2 chicken breasts, boneless or bone-in
- 1 carrot, sliced thin
- 2 medium potatoes, cubed
- 1 cup green beans or cubed zucchini
- 1 large onion, chopped
- seasoning options: salt, pepper, rosemary, thyme, parsley, minced ginger, soy sauce

Serves 2.

Preparation
Oil two sheets of aluminum foil. Place one breast on each. Top with the vegetables, season to taste, then seal the foil packets. Cook in coals for 30 minutes.

Quicky Pizza

Ingredients
- tortillas, sandwich wraps, or pittas
- pizza sauce
- cheese, grated
- topping options: pepperoni, cooked bacon, Italian sausage, deli ham, sliced tomato, chopped bell peppers, onions, mushrooms, etc.

Preparation
Assemble pizzas. They may be cooked over a stove or campfire in a covered pan. (Lightly oil the surface first.) Or wrap in foil and place on top of coals for 10–15 minutes. Do not put coals on top. Toppings of peppers, onions, or sausage must be precooked in a pan with a bit of oil.

Spider Dogs

Cut both ends of a hot dog in quarters lengthwise, leaving about 2 inches in the middle uncut. Use a forked stick or a long-handled cooking fork to spear the dog from the side, in the uncut section. As you roast them over live flames, the ends will curl back. It's still just a hot dog, but it looks funny and young kids enjoy them.

Mud-Spuds

A medium-size potato takes about an hour to bake when covered with coals. You can wrap them in foil, or try baking them in mud. Have the kids mix up some "clean" mud from pure mineral soil with no pebbles or vegetable matter. (Clayey soil is best.) They'll have to experiment to get the right consistency so that they can coat the potato with mud about $\frac{1}{2}$ inch thick. Cover the mud-spuds with coals and wait an hour. The mud will be hard. Crack them open and eat only the "meat" of the potato, leaving the skin.

Planning

Gear

Techniques

Hazards

Hiking

Camping with Kids

DESSERTS

Sticky Stick Apples

Ingredients
- apple
- cinnamon sugar

Preparation
Spit an apple on a stick and turn over hot coals until the skin becomes loose. Peel the skin off then roll the apple in cinnamon sugar. Cook over the coals again, turning regularly until the sugar melts. Eat while warm.

Bananasmores

Ingredients
- banana
- mini-marshmallows
- chocolate chips

Preparation
Slit the banana open lengthwise, leaving the peel on and intact along the bottom edge. Gently open the banana and cram it with the mini-marshmallows and chocolate chips. Wrap in aluminum foil and place on coals for 15 minutes. Eat with a spoon.

Alternative Preparation
You may substitute full-size marshmallows and chocolate bars, cutting them into small pieces.

PIE-IRON DISHES

From a child's point of view, a pie iron is an all-purpose cooking device, entirely sufficient for breakfast, lunch, supper, and dessert. As long as you can put it between two slices of bread, most kids will eat it if they cook it themselves in a pie iron. Dense whole-grain breads are best, but fluffy white bread works fine. Here are fillings to consider, some of which must be precooked:
- deli meat and cheese
- tuna and cheese
- beef steak or boneless chicken breast with barbecue sauce
- cheeseburgers
- pizza sauce, cheese, and pepperoni, ham, or bacon
- eggs (scrambled or hard-fried) with ham, bacon, or sausage
- peanut butter with marshmallow cream or jelly
- cream cheese and cinnamon sugar
- preserves or fruit pie filling

Once a child has mastered basic pie-iron technique, he can try dishes involving two or more steps. Fry a hamburger or egg in the iron, then use it in a pie-iron-cooked sandwich. Bake a single serving of cornbread or biscuit dough in the iron, then make a pie-iron meat pie. It's less efficient than other cooking methods, but that's not the point. The kid is having fun, learning a new skill, and accepting responsibility. What more could you ask for?

REFERENCE

Checklists

CLOTHING

- [ ] base layer (underwear, long underwear, leggings)
- [ ] insulation layer (shirt, pants, shorts, sweater, fleece jacket)
- [ ] exterior layer, outer shell (raingear, wind breaker, parka)
- [ ] socks (two layers)
- [ ] hiking boots
- [ ] in-camp footgear (sneakers, moccasins, sandals)
- [ ] water shoes, sandals
- [ ] hats (for sun, cold)
- [ ] gloves/mittens
- [ ] bandana
- [ ] swimsuit
- [ ] head net, bug suit

SHELTER AND SLEEP

- [ ] tent
- [ ] ground cloth, footprint
- [ ] tent seam sealer
- [ ] tent repair kit
- [ ] spare stakes
- [ ] stake mallet
- [ ] sleeping bag
- [ ] sleeping pad
- [ ] pillow
- [ ] cot
- [ ] tarp/kitchen fly
- [ ] screen house
- [ ] hammock
- [ ] folding chair, table
- [ ] whisk broom, dust pan
- [ ] entry mat

KITCHEN

- [ ] stove
- [ ] fuel
- [ ] funnel
- [ ] fuel filter
- [ ] windscreen
- [ ] stove repair kit/spares
- [ ] matches, lighters
- [ ] tinder, fire paste
- [ ] charcoal briquettes, firewood
- [ ] fire grate, barbecue grill
- [ ] fire pan
- [ ] water bottle, hydration bladder
- [ ] collapsible water jug
- [ ] water filter/purifier
- [ ] water filter spares
- [ ] cook pot with lid
- [ ] frying pan
- [ ] coffee pot
- [ ] pot grip, potholder
- [ ] reflector oven
- [ ] Dutch oven
- [ ] pie iron
- [ ] strainer
- [ ] plates, bowls
- [ ] cups, mugs
- [ ] cutlery
- [ ] spatula, stirring/serving spoon, tongs
- [ ] chef's knife, paring knife
- [ ] vegetable peeler
- [ ] skewers, toasting fork
- [ ] cutting board
- [ ] measuring cup
- [ ] corkscrew
- [ ] can opener
- [ ] ice chest
- [ ] aluminum foil
- [ ] paper towels
- [ ] camp soap, dish scrubber
- [ ] dishpan
- [ ] trash bags
- [ ] zip-lock bags
- [ ] bear bag, bearproof container
- [ ] kitchen stand/caddie/chuck box

ON THE MOVE

- ☐ maps, general and topographic
- ☐ compass
- ☐ pencil, straightedge
- ☐ GPS
- ☐ locator beacon
- ☐ watch
- ☐ altimeter
- ☐ daypack, waist pack
- ☐ stuff sacks
- ☐ trekking poles, hiking stick
- ☐ child carrier
- ☐ bear bell
- ☐ bear repellent
- ☐ camping permit
- ☐ fire permit
- ☐ reservations documents
- ☐ guidebook
- ☐ gaiters
- ☐ rain cover for backpack
- ☐ tools and spares for bike, boat, car, or RV
- ☐ hose, cables for RV hookups

FIRST-AID KIT

- ☐ adhesive bandages
- ☐ gauze
- ☐ nonstick sterile pads
- ☐ cotton swabs
- ☐ medical tape
- ☐ elastic bandage
- ☐ moleskin
- ☐ pain relievers
- ☐ antiseptic
- ☐ antibacterial ointment
- ☐ burn ointment
- ☐ eye drops
- ☐ snake-bite kit
- ☐ antihistamine
- ☐ epinephrine injector (e.g., EpiPen)
- ☐ antacids
- ☐ rehydration salts
- ☐ ipecac syrup
- ☐ anti-itch cream
- ☐ barrier cream for poisonous plants
- ☐ bandage shears
- ☐ tweezers
- ☐ razor blade, scalpel
- ☐ finger, toe splint
- ☐ flexible splint (e.g., SAM Splint)
- ☐ chemically reactive cold pack
- ☐ magnifying glass
- ☐ irrigation syringe
- ☐ medical gloves
- ☐ oral thermometer
- ☐ personal medications, prescription drugs
- ☐ first-aid guide

OTHER HEALTH AND HYGIENE

- ☐ toilet paper
- ☐ portable toilet with waste bags, chemicals
- ☐ sunblock
- ☐ zinc oxide cream
- ☐ lip balm
- ☐ sunglasses
- ☐ spare eyeglasses/contact lenses
- ☐ contact lens cleaning solution
- ☐ bug dope
- ☐ area insect repellent
- ☐ trowel
- ☐ personal toiletries kit
  - toothbrush, paste, floss
  - camp soap
  - towel
  - washrag
  - nail clipper
  - hairbrush, comb
  - sanitary napkins, tampons

TOOLS AND SURVIVAL

- ☐ knife
- ☐ multi-tool
- ☐ axe
- ☐ sharpening stone
- ☐ saw
- ☐ trowel, entrenching tool
- ☐ handheld UHF radio
- ☐ weather radio
- ☐ rope, light cordage
- ☐ duct tape
- ☐ clothes pins
- ☐ sewing kit
- ☐ flashlight, headlamp
- ☐ batteries, bulb for flashlight
- ☐ lantern
- ☐ batteries, fuel, mantles for lantern
- ☐ candles
- ☐ light sticks
- ☐ binoculars
- ☐ repair kit
  - wire
  - wire cutter pliers
  - tent pole repair sleeve
  - sewing kit
  - safety pins

- zipper pulls
- cordage
- air mattress patch kit
- boot adhesive
- ☐ survival kit
  - signal mirror
  - whistle
  - knife, razor blade
  - miniature flashlight, chemical light stick
  - fire-starter (sparker, lighter, matches, tinder, fuel tablets)
  - wire
  - parachute cord, string
  - fishing kit
  - compass
  - iodine tablets
  - energy bar
  - salt tablets
  - small plastic bag
  - cup
  - shelter: trash bag, emergency poncho, emergency blanket
  - first-aid basics: bandages, antiseptic, antibiotic ointment, painkiller

FUN AND MISCELLANEOUS

- ☐ games, toys, puzzles
- ☐ books, magazines
- ☐ hobby equipment
- ☐ pen, pencil, paper, journal
- ☐ nature guide
- ☐ fishing gear, license
- ☐ camera
- ☐ bike, helmet

Resources

WEBSITES

American Hiking Society (www.americanhiking.org): national organization promoting hiking

Appalachian Mountain Club (www.outdoors.org): promote outdoor recreation in the Appalachian region and throughout the East Coast

Campmor (www.campmor.com): extensive selection of general camping gear

GORP (www.gorp.com): general camping information, oriented toward backpackers

The Mountaineers (www.mountaineers.org): promote outdoor recreation in the Northwest

Parks Canada (www.pc.gc.ca/eng/index. aspx): information on all national parks, conservation areas and historic sites

Parks Canada Campground Reservation Service (www.pccamping.ca/parkscanada/): campsite availability and booking facility

Recreation.gov: information about federal nature and outdoor recreation facilities

Reserve America (www.reserveamerica. com): booking facility for federal, state, and private campgrounds and campsites

Toporama (http://atlas.nrcan.gc.ca/site/english/maps/topo/map): topographic map generator for Canada

U.S. Geological Survey (www.usgs.gov): topo maps and federal camping land maps

Wilderness Medicine Training Center (www.wildmedcenter.com): wilderness medicine instructional programs

Wildfoods.info: information about identifying and preparing wild plant foods

Woodall's (www.woodalls.com): camping information, oriented toward RVs

BOOKS

Angier, Bradford, and David K. Foster, *Field Guide to Edible Wild Plants*. Stackpole Books, 2008

Auerback, Paul S., *Medicine for the Outdoors: The Essential Guide to Emergency Medical Procedures and First Aid*, 5th ed. Mosby-Saunders, 2009

Berger, Karen, *Backpacking & Hiking*. DK Publishing, 2005

Bridge, Raymond, *Bike Touring: The Sierra Club Guide to Travel on Two Wheels*, 2nd ed. Sierra Club Books, 2009

Jacobson, Cliff, *Canoeing & Camping Beyond the Basics*, 3rd ed. Falcon Guides, 2007

Jacobson, Don, *The One Pan Gourmet: Fresh Food on the Trail*, 2nd ed. McGraw-Hill, 2005

Johnson, Richard, *Rich Johnson's Guide to Wilderness Survival*. McGraw-Hill, 2008

Kesselheim, Alan, *Trail Food: Drying and Cooking Food for Backpacking and Paddling*. McGraw-Hill, 1998

Mills, Sheila, *The Outdoor Dutch Oven Cookbook*, 2nd ed. McGraw-Hill, 2008

Moeller, Bill, and Jan Moellen, *The Complete Book of Boondock RVing: Camping Off the Beaten Path*. McGraw-Hill, 2007

Pewtherer, Michael, *Wilderness Survival Handbook: Primitive Skills for Short-Term Survival and Long-Term Comfort*. McGraw-Hill, 2010

Seidman, David, and Paul Cleveland, *The Essential Wilderness Navigator: How to Find Your Way in the Great Outdoors*, 2nd ed. McGraw-Hill, 2000

Woodall's Publications Corp., *Woodall's North American Campground Directory*. Woodall's, 2012

Glossary

bag liner: a lightweight fabric bag placed inside a sleeping bag for additional warmth and to keep it clean

base layer (wicking layer): layer of clothing worn against the body designed to wick moisture away from skin

baseplate (orienteering) compass: a compass consisting of a magnetic needle in a rotating capsule mounted on a clear plastic base

bear bag: a fabric bag with associated rigging to store food out of reach of bears and other animals

bear bell: a bell attached to clothing or a backpack to warn bears of a hiker's approach

bearing: the compass direction toward any object or destination

bivouac: to camp outside of an established campsite with minimal or no site preparation

bivy/bivy sack: a waterproof bag into which one places a sleeping bag and inside of which one sleeps, as on bivouac; used in lieu of a tent

blaze: a permanent mark to indicate a foot trail

boondocking: RV camping outside of an established campground and without utility hookups

compression sack: a stuff sack with attached straps and buckles to reduce the volume of a sleeping bag during transport, as when backpacking

contour line: a (usually curving) line on a topographic map connecting adjacent points of equal elevation. The **contour interval** is the vertical distance represented by each line.

cryptosporidium ("crypto"): a waterborne protozoan that causes the disease cryptosporidiosis

deadman: a buried anchor for a tent corner or guyline; used in soft ground where stakes do not hold

declination: the difference, measured in degrees, between true and magnetic north at any location on the earth's surface. Known as **variation** to boaters

DEET: N,N-Diethyl-meta-toluamide, the active chemical in most insect repellents for personal application

direction-of-travel arrow: a marking on a baseplate compass indicating the direction to travel, either in the field or on a map

Duluth pack (portage pack): a canvas backpack lacking a suspension system and popular among traditional canoeists. Although it is a trademarked name, the term is in general use for this style of pack.

Dutch oven: cast iron or aluminum cooking pot with short tripod legs and a recessed lid capable of holding burning coals

fifth-wheel camper: an RV trailer towed from a hitch installed on the bed of a pickup truck over the rear axle

flatwater: lakes and rivers without strong currents and obstacles. The opposite is **whitewater:** rivers with strong currents and obstacles.

fly: a tarp or other sheet material used for weather protection and set up so as not to be in direct contact with the ground. A **rain fly** is the outer wall of a double-wall tent.

footprint: a ground cloth made to fit the size and shape of a particular tent

gate (also, shed): red area printed on the bottom of a baseplate compass's rotating capsule coinciding with North on the dial

gear loft: a fabric panel attached inside a tent, near the top, that serves as a shelf for lightweight gear

giardia lamblia ("giardia"): a waterborne protozoan that causes the disease giardiasis

gorp: trail mix. A snack composed of various loose ingredients, but often including several of the following: nuts, peanuts, dried fruit, sunflower seeds, M&M candies.

GPS: in popular terms, a GPS is an electronic navigation device that calculates position, speed, distance, etc., using signals from Earth satellites. In literal terms, the **Geostationary Positioning System** is the network of satellites, and the navigation device is a **GPS receiver**.

grid north: north according to the grid imposed on a map. Usually only slightly different from true north, it can often be ignored and is frequently omitted from topographic maps.

ground cloth: a sheet of plastic or waterproof fabric used to protect a tent floor or to serve as the floor of a floorless tent

gunwale: the long strengthening members along the upper edges of a canoe's hull

guyline: a rope that holds down a part of a tent or fly and is not attached to a corner

hatchet: a small axe meant to be used with one hand

hydration bladder: a container for drinking water consisting of a durable plastic bag with a hose attached, through which water is sucked. Backpacks with a special compartment for a hydration bladder are **hydration-compatible**.

hypothermia: a serious medical condition in which the body's core temperature falls below 95°F

index line (lubber line): on a baseplate compass, the end of the direction-of-travel arrow opposite that of the arrow head, against which the bearing on the rotating dial may be read

kindling: small sticks and other burnable materials used to ignite fuel wood in a campfire

layering: a system of clothing in which separate layers perform different functions to keep the body dry and warm

lensatic compass: a compass with a sight and a pivoting lens that permits the object being sighted (the destination) and the compass bearing to be seen simultaneously

locator beacon: a handheld electronic device that sends an emergency message via an Earth-circling satellite

lockback: a folding knife with a mechanism that prevents the blade from accidentally folding into the case

magnetic north: the location on the Earth's surface of the magnetic north pole and toward which the north needle of a magnetic compass points. It does not coincide with the geographic (true) north pole.

microporous membrane: a layer in clothing, especially in raingear and boots, that prevents liquid water from entering but permits water vapor to escape

midship (*adj:* amidships): the area midway between the bow and stern (front and back) of a boat, canoe, etc.

moleskin: a synthetic material, smooth on one side and self-adhesive on the other, used to prevent foot blisters caused by friction of the skin against the boot or sock

motorhome: a self-propelled RV, in which the living quarters are attached to and accessible from the driver's compartment

nature scope: a child's optical instrument combining the functions of a telescope and a microscope

orienting lines: parallel lines etched on the bottom of the rotating capsule of a baseplate compass, allowing the dial to be aligned accurately with the grid of a map

pannier: bags attached beside a bicycle's wheels, in which cargo is carried

pie iron: a cooking instrument used over a campfire, consisting of a pair of hinged, hollow cast-metal plates attached to long handles

pitch: to set up a tent

planisphere: a device for identifying stars in the sky

pop-up camper: a small RV trailer with a roof and sides that collapse for ease of towing and storage

quinzhee: an emergency shelter consisting of a cavity dug into a mound of snow

reflector oven: a heat reflector made from folding or collapsing sections of sheet metal, used for baking in front of a campfire

RV: recreational vehicle. A "home on wheels" that may be either trailered behind a tow vehicle or self-propelled.

scale: the ratio between a dimension on a map and the distance it represents on the ground

scat: feces left by wild animals

scree: an extensive area of small, loose rocks on the side of a hill

shell: outerwear clothing that provides protection from wind and precipitation

spork: a combination spoon and fork

strike: to take down a tent or pack up and leave a campsite

stuff sack: a fabric bag in which gear is carried, especially a sleeping bag or tent

thwart: a strengthening cross-member extending between opposite gunwales on a canoe

tinder: easily burnable material used to start a fire

topographic map ("topo"): a map that shows the topography, or slopes, of a terrain by means of contour lines

travel trailer: an RV trailer other than a pop-up camper or a fifth-wheel camper

treeline: the elevation on a mountain above which trees do not grow

true north: the Earth's geographic north pole (i.e., the north end of the Earth's axis of rotation) or the direction along the Earth's surface leading to that place

tump line: a strap on a backpack meant to be worn around the forehead

ultralight: a style of backpacking in which all unnecessary weight is eliminated

urushiol: an oily, allergenic substance found in poison ivy, poison oak, and poison sumac

wannigan: a box for carrying gear, designed to fit into a canoe

wicking: capillary action in clothing fibers serving to draw moisture away from the skin

windage: the exposed surface area of a boat against which wind may act to impede progress or make control difficult

Index

...ning Bible

Notes